DOGMAN TERROR IN THE WOODS

TIFFANY S. DORAN

FOREWORD

BRIAN KING-SHARP

In the vast expanse of nature's embrace, where the untamed wilderness whispers its secrets, some stories defy explanation and challenge our perception of reality. Within this realm, my dear friend Tiffany fearlessly ventures, delving into the depths of the unknown and bringing forth a tale that will leave you breathless and questioning the boundaries of our understanding.

As the host of the renowned podcast *Sasquatch Odyssey*, I have shared the airwaves with Tiffany and her husband, Zack, as they recounted their extraordinary encounters with the enigmatic Bigfoot. Their stories have captivated audiences worldwide, igniting a curiosity and wonder that lingers long after the last word is spoken. Now, Tiffany takes her passion for the unexplained to new heights with her latest book, *Dogman Terror in the Woods*.

Within the pages of this gripping tale, Tiffany weaves a narrative that intertwines the struggles of two couples with the menacing presence of Dogman and Bigfoot on their property. Drawing from her own experiences and the countless stories shared by those who have encountered these elusive creatures, Tiffany creates a world where fear and survival dance hand in hand and the line between reality and nightmare blurs.

What sets *Dogman Terror in the Woods* apart is the raw authenticity that permeates every page. Tiffany's ability to seamlessly blend fact and fiction is a testament to her unwavering dedication to the truth and her remarkable storytelling prowess. As you immerse yourself in this tale, you will question the boundaries of what we perceive as real and the unseen forces that may lurk beyond our comprehension.

But this book is more than just a thrilling narrative. It is a testament to the resilience of the human spirit, the unyielding determination to confront the unknown, and the bonds of love and friendship that can withstand even the most harrowing of trials. Through the characters' struggles, Tiffany explores the depths of human courage and the lengths we are willing to go to protect those we hold dear.

As you embark on this journey through the pages of *Dogman Terror in the Woods*, prepare to be transported to a world where danger lurks in the shadows and the unseen forces of nature hold sway. Tiffany's vivid descriptions and masterful storytelling will envelop you in an atmosphere of suspense and intrigue, leaving you on the edge of your seat, eagerly turning each page to uncover the next twist in the tale.

I am honored to have witnessed the evolution of this book, from the initial spark of inspiration to its completion. I have seen the passion and dedication that Tiffany has poured into her research and, now, into the creation of this captivating story. It is a testament to her unwavering belief in the existence of these mysterious beings and her commitment to sharing her own experiences with the world.

Through her appearances in *Sasquatch Odyssey*, Tiffany has become a trusted voice in the realm of the unexplained. Her willingness to open up and share her personal encounters with Bigfoot has not only captivated audiences but also provided solace and validation to those who have had similar experiences. Now, with *Dogman Terror in the Woods*, Tiffany expands her storytelling prowess to encompass the chilling presence of Dogman and Bigfoot, creatures that have long haunted the fringes of folklore and urban legends.

In this book, Tiffany skillfully weaves together the narratives of two couples who find themselves thrust into a battle for survival against the menacing forces of Dogman and Bigfoot. As the tension mounts and the characters are pushed to their limits, Tiffany's vivid descriptions and attention to detail will transport you deep into the heart of the wilderness, where every rustle of leaves and snap of twigs become a harbinger of danger.

But beyond the thrills and chills, *Dogman Terror in the Woods* is a testament to the power of storytelling itself. It is a reminder that within the realm of fiction, we can explore the depths of our fears, confront the unknown, and ultimately find strength and resilience in the face of adversity. Tiffany's ability to craft a narrative that resonates with readers on both an emotional and intellectual level is a testament to her skill as a storyteller.

As you embark on this journey through the pages of *Dogman Terror in the Woods*, prepare to be enthralled, to have your heart race with anticipation, and to question the boundaries of what we perceive as reality. Tiffany's unique blend of personal encounters, research, and imagination will leave you questioning the unseen forces that may lurk just beyond our understanding.

I am honored to have the opportunity to introduce you to this remarkable work. Tiffany's dedication to her craft, her unwavering belief in the existence of these creatures, and her ability to transport readers into a world where the extraordinary becomes tangible are truly commendable. *Dogman Terror in the Woods* is a testament to her passion, her talent, and her commitment to sharing stories that push the boundaries of our imagination.

So, dear reader, prepare yourself for an unforgettable journey. Open your mind, embrace the unknown, and allow Tiffany's words to guide you through the chilling encounters with Dogman and Bigfoot that await you in the pages of this extraordinary book.

Now sit back, relax, and enjoy the ride.

Brian King-Sharp
Founder & CEO Paranormal World Productions, LLC

Creator/Host:
Sasquatch Odyssey Podcast
True Crime Odyssey Podcast
Weird Encounters Podcast
Disturbing History Podcast

1

A new day, a new time, a fresh start. That's what we needed. Living life in the big city full of smog, noisy streets full of bustling cars and blaring horns, not to mention bad attitudes on every corner, just wasn't working out for us any longer. We had lived that life for almost twenty years, and it was time for something better that we knew was out there. My wife and I always visited the mountains when we went on vacation. We both loved to hike, fish, and hunt. Coming back home was always depressing. Well, I guess if we're being honest, no one likes to come home from vacation. But for us, there was always an ache in our soul until we could get back out there. Nonetheless, we would come home to our corporate jobs and just push through, all the while, planning for the next trip.

We sat down at dinner one night after work, tired and downtrodden and we made the decision to move as soon as possible. We sat there and planned the whole thing out. We were thrilled to finally be able to leave. We looked all over, hoping to find a cabin nestled in the heart of the forest with hiking trails, small and big game to hunt, as well as a water source to be able to fish. I guess our dream overtook reality. We didn't find that cabin nestled in the heart of the forest with any of those things. But we did find a nice three-bedroom ranch

TIFFANY S. DORAN

home that fit all our needs about two miles out of the woods on a dead-end road.

No neighbors in sight, no smog or blaring horns, and no bad attitudes to find, well, unless they were our own. We had a large expanse of land attached to the rear of our home and we also purchased the empty lot beside it to ensure that no one else would be able to build on it. This was all ours and we wanted to finally be able to live the proverbial dream, just me and my wife. About five miles down the road, was a farm. We enjoyed taking walks in the evening and one night we walked further than normal and that's when we found it. The owners were working outside, so we walked over and introduced ourselves.

"Hello," I said as I walked over smiling. I reached out my hand to shake his. "My name is Mark, and this is my wife, Contessa. It's nice to meet you."

My wife interjected. "You can call Connie; she said as she stuck her hand out to shake theirs as well.

"Hi, I'm always glad to meet new people, I'm Marie and this is my husband, John. I love your name," Marie said. "I can't say that I have ever heard it before."

I knew then that my wife and Marie would hit it off well. We had told them that we had recently purchased the home up the road and how we had some land and would love to have something like they had for ourselves. They had endless rows of corn, a smaller garden off to the side of their home for other produce like, lettuce, carrots, potatoes, etc. They seemed to have had it all. They were fully sustained without having to take any trips into town to go to the grocery store.

John and Marie were kind, well mannered, and driven. In their early fifties, they're lives revolved around family and farming.

Marie was more than excited to take my wife to show her around their garden and my wife was more than excited to go. John and I stood leaned up against the cow gate staring off into the distance at the mountains.

"So, John, how's the hunting here," I asked. "Any good-sized game to be had?"

2

"Well, not too bad," he said as he repositioned his ball cap. "You have your deer here, some grouse, rabbits if that's your thing, enough I would say. We also live off our animals. So, we have the meat from our cows and chickens that we harvest and fresh eggs every morning. I don't really do too much hunting. I mean, I do on occasion if I get a craving for some deer meat. But I would think if you're primarily going to be hunting for your meats, then there is enough to sustain you and your wife here for sure. Do you guys like to fish, too?"

"We absolutely do, John. Is there any good fishing around here then since you mentioned it?"

John sighed and took his hat off and turned to faced me. "Well yeah, really good fishing to be had but you have to be careful."

"Careful of what, John? Cliffs, rolling rocks, terrain," I asked confused by how serious he suddenly became. "Is it unsafe to traverse?"

He chuckled. "I wish that were all it was, friend."

Just then Marie came walking back over with Connie, changing the mood and conversation altogether.

"What are you guys over here so serious about?" Marie asked.

"Just guy stuff honey", John said as he leaned over and kissed her cheek. "Just guy stuff."

I was still curious about what John was talking about but didn't push the envelope. We had just met so I didn't want to overstep my bounds seeing as how he could turn out to be a great friend and his wife, a great friend to mine. So, we finished our pleasantries upon leaving and walked home before it got dark. Connie was childlike as she talked to me about everything Marie had shared with her. I was happy to see her smiling again, finally. This was my wife. This was who I married. Not the woman I lived with in the city. Peace had absolutely found her again and I couldn't be more glad. I was puzzled though, about what John was talking about so I decided that night after I showered, that we would go out the next day and look around. We woke up around six that next morning, had coffee and breakfast and got geared up to go hiking in the woods.

"This is going to be great," Connie exclaimed, "It feels like it's been so long since we've been able to do this!"

I looked over at her and smiled. "Want to know the best part, "We can do this anytime we want to now. We're not tied down to schedules, a clock, any of that."

We walked for a while taking everything in. The trees seemed so tall here, and the brush was so thick. The terrain wasn't bad. It was a little rocky but easily passable for hiking.

"The hunting will be interesting though with everything so grown up. Anything could hide in here and we wouldn't be able to see it. It would definitely be something we would need a tree stand for to see anything small." I told Connie.

She had stopped to take a drink of her water and wipe the sweat from her face. "Yes, I was thinking the same thing. I think we need to find a good tree for that while we're out here scouting."

We stood listening to the sounds of the forest. Birds were singing but off in the distance a way, twigs began to snap and crack.

Connie and I unholstered our weapons. This was new territory for us, so we had no idea what to expect. Could that be a deer or a bear? It sounded heavy enough to be either. We crouched down and began slowly walking forward, doing our best to be as quiet as possible. As we approached the sound, we were met with a tall, thick bramble of brush. We couldn't see all the way through it, just enough to tell color. It was brown and appeared to be on the larger side.

"I bet that's a bear." Connie whispered.

"I would agree," I said, "Just based off color and the sizeable steps taken."

We slowly retreated backward the way we came since there wasn't anything large enough to take down a bear if it charged us in our packs. A bear is something there wasn't enough protection for. That was something we didn't really think about, honestly. John hadn't mentioned seeing any bears out here. Maybe that's what he meant when he said the fishing is good, but we should be careful. Connie and I made it out of the brush, walked all the way around and then back down to ensure we were far enough away so that the bear couldn't scent us near. That's when we saw it.

A small river at the base of the hill we had just trekked down.

"Mark this in your gps," Connie told me. "We didn't bring our poles, but I bet there is a great number of fish in here. We can always come back later and go fishing."

I stood there watching the water run over the rocks, elated to be there and happy that this is now our home. We suddenly heard those heavy footfalls again. Connie whipped her head around trying to tell its direction. I pulled out my weapon ready to fire just in case. I could at least injure whatever that was. A horrible stench filled the air just then. Almost like rotten fish and a dead animal intertwined into one foul odor all its own.

"I don't remember smelling anything like that near that bear we saw earlier, assuming it was a bear, Connie," I said whispering to her. "This has to be something else."

Connie looked concerned. "Well what else could it be, Mark, it must be that bear or at least a different one. The only thing is, is if it's a bear, it's sick, no doubt about it. It almost smells like a portion of its decaying or maybe that's a severe infection we're smelling. Either way, we need to get out of here. If it is some type of rabid animal, they are unpredictable at best. Just make sure the coordinates are marked and let's get out of here."

We left the water behind and made our way back towards home. Once we were away from the thick brush and rotten stench, we slowed down our pace.

"Well, I can honestly say that was the weirdest hike we've ever had." I said.

Connie stopped and took a drink from her water bottle. "Yeah, I would agree. Next time we come up here, we need bear spray and our bigger rifle. I still have no idea what was bringing that smell on, but it was terrible."

"Yes, I'll give you that. I don't think I have ever smelled something so foul. Let me ask you this though, did you feel some kind of unease at that river?" I asked Connie.

Connie looked at me puzzled. "You mean like, scared, was I scared while we were at the river?"

I sighed, "Well, I guess in a way but, it was just an unsettling feeling that came over me after I pulled out my gun. It was almost like I would regret it if I fired. I don't know, maybe it was just me."

We made our way back home, had lunch, and started planning and measuring everything for our garden.

The next evening, we met with John and Marie at their house for dinner and went over everything they had done to ensure all their vegetables would survive not only in the harsh summers but also the cold winters as well. Little did I know, John owned all that land surrounding his home as far as the eye could see. Over dessert, we talked about the weird day we had before when we went scouting the land. We had told them of the possible bear sighting, finding the river, and that awful stench. John leaned back in his chair and laid his fork on the plate.

"Smell," he asked, "You smelled something?

"Yeah," I said, "It was almost like partial decay mixed with rotten fish."

"Do you think it was just the smell of all the fish that was there in the water?" Marie asked.

"No ma'am," Connie spoke up, "This wasn't just a normal fish smell. We've fished for over a decade, and I can assure you that it wasn't coming from fish that were swimming. This was almost like leaving fish that you just cleaned lying on the table in sweltering heat for a few days. It was foul."

John cut his eyes at Marie who instantly looked down at her pie on the plate. "You know what I think it is," John said to Marie.

Marie rolled her eyes at John. Me and Connie felt awkward at that moment.

"I know what you think it is, John, but I'm telling you, that doesn't even exist. Not here, not anywhere." Marie said wiping her mouth.

"But I saw it with my own eyes, Marie." John said sternly.

"If ya'll will excuse me, Marie said, dismissing what was just said, I'm going to go do the dishes."

"Here, I'll help you." Connie said, as she stood from the table.

Me and John sat in awkward silence after the girls left the room. I didn't know what to say at that point and I think he was partly thinking he had said too much. I could hear them in the kitchen talking. I couldn't make out what was being said though. I took a long drink of my beer and as I sat it back on the table, John spoke up.

"I guess you're wondering what all that was about huh, Mark." He said as he glanced over at me.

"Well, I wasn't going to pry, that's not my business. That's between you and your wife." I said.

"Come on," John said as he stood up, "Let's go sit on the front deck."

We walked past the kitchen and Marie once again threw a sideways glance at John. Connie smiled, winked, and gave a small shrug of the shoulders. The evening was perfect for sitting out in a rocking chair talking with a friend. The sky was starlit with an indigo backdrop which illuminated the stars that much more.

John took a long drink of his beer and sat it down at his feet. "I guess you really do need to know what's going on. Marie and I talked it over after you and Connie left that first night. She was adamant against it because she doesn't believe in it and she doesn't want me to scare people off but I'm telling you, it's real. That's why the last family left. I'm surprised they took the time to pack."

I cleared my throat and took a drink. "What exists or doesn't exist and I'm assuming scared off the last family that lived in the home we're in now, what has Marie ready to smack you silly in there?"

John was quiet for a minute. He almost looked like he was searching for the right words to say. He finally looked over at me and said something I wouldn't have ever thought.

"Dog man, Mark, there's a dog man that lives in these woods. It's on your property up the road as well as ours. I've seen it several times. The family that used to live in your home and on that property, were being terrorized. It would take it's claws and drag them down the sides of the house every night. Did you see the fresh paint out there, Mark, that's why it's there. They had to fix it up before they could sell it. The man used to go hunting with me when I decided to go. That's when we saw it and that's when he and I put two and two together

7

about what was going on at their house. Marie wants to slap me silly because she doesn't believe me. She thinks that family moving was because I filled their head with nonsense and scared them off."

I sat back in my chair and slowly started rocking. "A dog man huh," I said, "Well, I have to say I haven't ever heard of that before. You grow up hearing all kinds of folk tales from your dad and your grandpa, and I did. I heard all about bigfoot, Nessie, the jersey devil, you name it. But dog man, yes, that's a new one for me. Now, a story that my grandpa told me was that he was out hunting and had two bigfoots flanking him. He said he had one on either side of him almost escorting him out of the woods."

"Did you believe him, Mark?" John asked.

"Well sure, who doesn't believe stories their grandpa tells them. I went out every summer I was there and looked all over his property trying to find them or have some experience of my own. I mean, it never happened but I still believed him. He told me that sometimes these types of things only show themselves to who they want to see them, not to everyone. I just figured they didn't want me to see them for whatever reason."

"Well," John began, "If that's the case, I really wish this didn't want me to see it."

"Have you ever had any incidents here at your home, John?" He shook his head no as he took the last drink of his beer. "Not one, I don't know why this thing was hell bent on terrorizing them and not us. I'm glad it didn't or hasn't but there has to be some correlation, you know."

"Have you ever compared yours and Marie's life to theirs, like, is there something they had that you and Marie didn't at the time that may be bringing it in?" I asked.

"Well, no, I mean they had a dog, a few small children, and some chickens. But we have cows and chickens too." John said.

"The dog and the small children," I said, "That must be it. I can't be too sure with this dog man so to speak because I know nothing of it or it's habits. But let's hypothetically speak here and compare it to what I was told about bigfoot."

2

———————

John could be kind of intimidating at times, and this was one of those times so I was hoping I would make sense with what I said.

"Okay, let's hear it, I'm all ears." John said as he turned to face me.

"So, my grandpa told me several stories. He said that female bigfoot were drawn in by the laughter and squealing of children. He said it's because they're chemical make-up is so close to ours which leads me to believe that maybe toddler bigfoot sounds the same as our human children. Now, the males, like all males do, have that territorial gene. That goes for any other mammal they feel causes competition or who they feel would move into their terrain or, if they felt threatened by. What if by chance, that is what happened then?"

John sat silent and just looked at me. "I guess that could've been the case. I can tell you though that this was no bigfoot, this was sinister, evil if you will. It had the head of a canine, long snout. It had a large tuft of hair on the back of its neck, but the body of a man except the feet. The prints it left looked like dog prints. It was the scariest things I'd ever seen. But maybe that's why it was an every night attack with that family. Maybe the dog man didn't like the dog, or the children, or both."

"It's honestly hard to tell and if this dog man is what me and Connie saw, then we will just have to be on our toes more than normal out here." I said.

"I don't honestly know if there's any firepower that you guys could take with you that would even be able to protect you if you came across this beast, that's what concerns me. I don't know if anything will outside of a grenade." John said wringing his hands together.

Shortly after, Marie and Connie came out to join them. John cut his eyes at me as if to say conversation over for now and I caught on to it quickly.

"It sure is a beautiful night out here." Marie said as she sat down.

"It really is," Connie replied, "Almost a shame we have to head home."

I stood up to join my wife. "Yeah, time to go, it is getting late. I want to get to work first thing on the plans we worked out to start our garden. Thank you, guys, so much for everything. The information as well as dinner. It was all great and I look forward to seeing ya'll again soon."

On the ride home, Connie told me why Marie was so upset, and I shared with her what John had told me. Well, maybe not all of it. I told her just enough to where it would line up with what she heard from Marie. I didn't go into detail about the attacks on the house or any of that. I don't know how she would react to that, and he didn't want her to be afraid if something like this was going to start coming around again since they moved in. Who knows, maybe this beast thinks we're the same family that used to live here. We were almost back to the house and something large darted out in front of the car. I swerved to miss it and I just did. But it was a close call.

"What in the world was that Mark," Connie yelled. "Was that a bear?"

I hoped it was, but it ran so fast in front of us, it was all just a blur. A large furry blur. Our hearts were racing and when we got home, and we were timid to even get out of the car. I was thankful I had put the motion sensor light up however, because that was our only source of light down here near the woods.

"Listen honey, I want you to sit in the car, lock the doors, and don't move from it. I am going to go have a look around and open the house. When I signal you, I want you to run as fast as you can inside, understand?" I sternly asked her.

I grabbed my large halogen flashlight and got out. I lit it up as bright as day out there. I didn't see anything around the car or the front of the house. My heart raced as I walked around the sides of the house to the backyard. We had so much land back there, whatever that was could be anywhere. Everything John and I talked about was ringing in my ears and it was causing me to panic even more. What if what that was, that ran in front of the car, was a dog man?

I heard Connie blaring the horn and I ran as fast as I could back to the front of the house.

I shone my light all around and didn't see anything. I ran to the car, grabbed Connie and we both ran in as fast as our legs would take us.

"I saw it Mark, I don't think that was a bear. It was big, tall, and looked like a werewolf. But they don't exist. Werewolves are only in the movies, so what was that in the woods? Connie asked frantically.

I was afraid it would be a dog man and based off her description compared to what John told me, that's exactly what it sounded like.

I was in a position at that moment, that I knew I had no choice but to tell Connie the remainder of mine and John's conversation.

"I know that you said Marie was upset and no doubt, she's just afraid she's going to lose us as friends and neighbors because of what John told me. Marie said these things don't exist but now you know by personal experience that they do. The family that lived here before us, were terrorized by what you just saw in the woods. John said he and the guy who lived here before, saw it a few times when they were out hunting. Marie thinks otherwise. She thinks John scared them off with tall tales. But that just wasn't the case."

Connie was silent. I know her mind must've been spinning by what I just told her. I couldn't do or say anything to make it make sense to her. Unfortunately, this was something that she would have to process the best way she could.

"Are you saying that we're in danger then, Mark," she asked. "Will this, what did you call it, dog man, do the same thing to us?"

"I couldn't tell you with any certainty, Connie. All I know is that we can't let it push us out of here the way it did the family before us. This is our home and we have worked too hard to finally get here. We are going to do everything we had planned before we saw this. John said that he and Marie haven't experienced anything negative. No attacks on their animals, no damage to their home, none of what this other family did."

I saw the anxiety in her face lessen a little after a while. "I wonder why though, Mark. Why this poor family and nothing for John and Marie. That doesn't make any sense to me."

I told her the previous family's living situation and how that could be what played a major role in this thing's behavior. I watched her completely calm down at that point, almost like it clicked with her. I could only assume she was thinking that we may be fine then since we have no children, dogs, or even farm animals right now.

"One thing is for sure, Mark," she said with determination in her voice, "You're right, this will not chase us away from our home, I won't let it. We are hunters. We have killed very large animals over the years and you and I can take this dog man down before I let it take our home."

I hadn't ever seen that side of her before. It was a different kind of grit and tension in her voice. She was in the mindset that this was war. I was proud of her for taking that attitude and not wanting to pack up and leave out of fear. She hasn't ever been a fearful person, but this dog man was straight of a nightmare. Seeing it at night, with its body slightly sticking out of the trees, made it worse. Its eyes glowed an amber color from what Connie had said. She said it stood on two feet, staring at her in the car. Its mouth was open, and she could see the large teeth. I laid in bed that night replaying what she said. A werewolf. I couldn't even believe that this type of thing existed. Where had it come from, is it the only one, are there more of them in the woods? There must be. We can't all be experiencing just one single dog man.

The next morning, we woke up early and set out to get all the plans we drew up the night before laid out. She and I both kept a watchful eye out for one another.

"Do we take a chance on getting any animals at this point?" Connie asked me as we looked at the blueprint for a place to put our chickens.

"We are going to do everything we have always planned. All we have to do is build everything up further and a little heavier to keep things out. We just beef up our normal precautions. That's all. I'm not letting this stop anything we've talked about."

"I really want to talk to Marie," Connie said as she and I gathered all the chicken wire. "She has to know that John is telling the truth and maybe, if it's coming from me, she'll believe it.

I knew that, that was a possibility. But getting someone to believe this would be easier said than done. If Marie doesn't believe in these things or any other cryptid, I don't know if Connie will be able to convince her either. Bit with that, I know Connie's mindset and she will do her absolute best.

"Look Marie, I know how ridiculous this sounds," Connie said at our house over dinner a few days later. "I also know it sounds like some halfcocked idea that came from some drunk hunters out in the woods one night. But I saw this thing, with my own eyes. I felt the fear it puts off. I have dreamed of it every night since I saw it. It is a real thing. John saw it, the previous neighbors saw it, and now we have too. John didn't run that poor family off, Marie. They were chased off that property from this dog man."

I was waiting for Marie to storm off from the table as she did before. She didn't though. She quietly sat there, looking at all of us. John reached over and laid his hand on her arm. You could see the wheels spinning.

"I don't expect you to instantly believe what we're saying Marie," John said, "I know that would be impossible and also unfair to you, all I'm asking is that you try to take this into consideration coming from me, and now our new friends."

Marie still wasn't saying anything. I felt bad for her, I really did. I almost felt like we were having a dog man intervention with her. I guess we really were though if you think about it. But I know this is a big pill to swallow. John was so sincere with her, and I could only hope that it would help her to be more open minded to this. Finally, Marie broke the silence that was hovering over us. It wasn't something any of us expected her to say.

"I know the stance I have taken;" she began. "But this is a stance I had to take though, a protection mechanism for myself. I know these creatures exist, I too have seen them, but not here and I've never told anyone, not even you, John and I'm sorry." She said.

Silence once again surrounded all of us as we sat stunned at what she just said.

"You've seen them," John asked. "Where, when?"

"I grew up on a farm; that you know. But I experienced one when I was out helping my mother hang up clothes on the line one morning. It either didn't know I was there or did and just didn't care. It was like seeing a tall German Shepard walking on two feet near the wood line by our house. I didn't know what it was or where it came from, but I was so afraid. I ran into the house leaving the clothes in the basket outside. My mother of course didn't believe me. The only thing I could do to even feel comfortable going back outside again, was to convince myself I was seeing things and that what I saw, didn't really exist."

"Did you see it anymore after that?" Connie asked.

"I did unfortunately. But it had been a few years from the first time I saw it. I was packing up my car and headed off to college and I saw it walking out of the woods carrying a deer. Once I left, I never looked back and swore to myself that I was only seeing things again. When John came to me about this, I instantly dismissed it because if not, the fear would only be dredged up again and I wouldn't feel comfortable living in my own home. I told myself that this creature everyone is seeing, must be a wolf. Just a normal, everyday wolf that is perfectly normal and natural to have. Dogmen don't exist and that's final."

As soon as she finished that sentence however, something

happened that couldn't be dismissed away. A loud scraping sound echoed through our house. I instantly thought of what John said about this beast scraping the sides of our house when the old neighbors lived here. Is that what that sound was, the claws from this dog man? Connie and I jumped up from the table. John ran to the windows to close them and make sure they were secure. Marie sat in fear at the table not moving. I ran and got two guns. One for me and one for John.

"Connie, you stay with Marie." I said making sure my gun was loaded. "John and I are going outside."

"I'm sorry," Connie said, "I think I misunderstood you; did you say that you guys were going outside? You yourself told me that this dog man used to do the same exact thing to the family who lived here before us. You said it drug it's claws across the house. Do you not think that's what that was just now and yet you two want to go outside with this thing? I know what I said about us being hunters and we are Mark, but you must be smart. We will take this animal down but loading up two small weapons and going out the door filled with anger, fear and testosterone, isn't smart."

John and I looked at each other, both caught off guard by her tone.

"Well, yeah, we're going outside" I said, trying to match her intensity. "We have to figure out what that sound was. We can only assume that's what it was, but we don't know for sure unless we go check."

Connie couldn't believe what she was hearing. "Look, I appreciate the stance you two are taking. You are the men, and you want to make sure me and Marie are okay. I get it but Mark, you didn't see what I saw that night coming out of the woods. You didn't see what John and Marie saw in the woods with their encounter either. This creature is big, and it is mean. It's not like any other animal that we have seen or taken down in the woods before. This dog man is not something that any weapon we have is going to take down. The only thing you're going to be successful at is making it even angrier than it already is. We are going to have formulate a plan, all of us together."

I holstered my gun and motioned for John to do the same. If we walked out that door now, the dog man would be the least of our worries.

"I can't lie, John started, "I didn't really want to go out there and face that thing again."

I just shook my head. I guess until I see this thing, I'm just not going to understand.

"Well, what do you propose we do then?' I asked everyone.

They all looked at each other and then back at me. "Well," Marie spoke up, "It's been quiet since that one sound. No movement, no more metallic scraping sounds, just the sounds of our voices talking. One thing I'm certain of," she continued, "Is that John and I are spending the night here. I am not walking out that door until the sun comes up."

Connie reached out her hand for Marie's. "Honey, you both are welcome to stay here anytime."

She stood up from the table and went to the linen closet and got extra pillows, sheets, and a blanket.

"The couch has a pull-out bed in it," I said as I made my way into the living room to show them. "It may not be the most comfortable but for one night it'll be fine."

"That'll be just fine, Mark. I appreciate yours and Connie's hospitality, I really do." John said as he shook my hand.

Connie came in the room carrying four pillows, the sheets and a large quilt. She began making the pull-out bed for them bed for them while I showed them where the towels were if they wanted to shower. We sat around that evening like a bunch of teenagers. We watched movies, had popcorn and soon, we all fell asleep. Connie woke me up a little after three in the morning to come to bed with her. I didn't even know she left the room. On the way to the bedroom, we heard a loud scream from outside.

Connie turned around, eyes wide and whispered to me, 'What the hell was that?"

"If I had to guess, I would say it could be a bobcat." I said. We're new here so we aren't too familiar with noises that happen in the overnight and honestly, we're never up at this hour. It could happen every night and we just don't know it."

I was trying to keep her calm. I could only hope I was right with what I told her. Who's to say I'm not. This whole dog man thing has everyone in an uproar and every little thing that happens is automatically because of that. We just all need to get back to normal somehow. The next morning, I woke up before everyone. I made coffee, breakfast, and set the table.

"Seven in the morning that's lazy for me," John said as he walked into the kitchen, "I'm usually up no later than five-thirty."

"Well, we were all up later than normal and tensions were high. So, you'll have to cut yourself some slack for that."

Just as John sat down, Connie and Marie both came in the kitchen at the same time. They both looked like they were still half asleep. I set the coffee pot and mugs on the kitchen table along with all the food.

"I dreamed of that monster all night," Marie said, "This is why I tried to convince myself it didn't exist all those years."

John looked at me and then back to Marie. I knew what he was feeling. I felt like I had to be the leader in this charge because I felt I would be more capable of carrying the level head in this situation since I haven't encountered it yet. Well, unless you want to count me almost hitting it with my car, that is. But it wasn't a good enough sighting to scare me out of my wits like everyone else was.

3

"I'm going outside Mark if you want to join me," John said after breakfast had been cleaned up, "I know I've seen these things in the daytime, just as Marie has, but I'm not going to be afraid to leave your house or mine."

Connie and Marie put up less of a fight today than they had last night. John and I cautiously walked outside, head on a swivel.

"It had to have come from our back lot," I said, "These woods you see off to the side really don't have much depth to them before it's just trees and a steep cliff. I wouldn't even call them woods. However, Connie said she saw it coming out of the woods so this would have to be where she saw it. No wonder she was blaring the horn. That was a close sighting of this thing."

I never doubted my wife, but until you are in the position the person is when they tell you about it, you can't really appreciate it.

"This is also the side the guy had to paint before they could sell the house. It had long scratches down and across the aluminum over here." John said pointing.

We walked to the side of the house where we heard the loud metallic scraping sound coming from. It was the same side John was just talking about. I fully expected to see large scratches in the aluminum that I would have to prime and paint or from the sounds of it, possibly replace altogether. Nothing. Not a mark one anywhere to be found. We went all around the perimeter of our house. There wasn't any evidence of damage whatsoever. John and I just looked at each other in bewilderment.

"That makes no sense. You were here, you heard it too. How can something that was so loud, that could've only been something dragging their nails across aluminum, have not left a mark?" I asked John.

"Your guess is as good as mine, I have no explanation for that one." He replied still in shock.

We started walking towards the furthest part of our back lot. We were looking for anything at this point. John and I split up to hopefully find something in a quicker time frame. There were some areas back there you could go back into a shallow portion of the woods. It was all grown up however and no human could get through. Connie and I ventured back there when we were getting everything set up that day for the animals and our gardens. There were briar bushes as tall as we were. That's of course not to say something like this dogmen couldn't get through. I'm assuming just like bigfoot; they go through all kinds of things, and it doesn't bother them.

So maybe whatever this was, did come from back there. Either way, it still didn't explain the sound we all heard last night. Two and two are not equaling four here and I don't like it at all. We don't have neighbors near us. We're not near any highways or machinery plants. Something was on our property last night. I don't believe in coincidences, and I totally believe that whatever I almost hit with my truck and this strange sound were connected somehow. I just have to prove it. Connie and Marie met us in the backyard, and I explained to both of them that the house had no damage on it at all. They also were shocked at that based on the sound. Connie and Marie started looking in the woods where we stood. Connie saw it first and gasped.

"Well, you got it right Mark, it was a bobcat." She said looking over at me while pointing into the wood line.

This bobcat lay lying on the ground surrounded by waist high briar bushes and me and John had completely missed it. I pushed the briars back as much as possible to take a closer look. It had been mauled, but eerily enough, the look that was frozen on its face was one of terror, shock, almost like it was caught off guard. Is this a thing in the animal world where they have such a look on their faces when they are attacked? That I don't know for sure but this bobcat, sure did appear to have been ambushed.

"We have to bury it," Marie said. "If not, you guys are going to have an even bigger problem."

John chuckled trying to lighten the mood. "Bigger than dog man?"

Luckily, I had left my post hole diggers out there and we buried the bobcat before making our way back up to the house to prevent any other critters from making a meal of it.

"Well, I feel we have overstayed our welcome at this point," John said, "Marie and I need to get back home and tend to our animals. No doubt they're raising cane wanting something."

After gathering all their things from inside, Connie gave Marie a hug. "You guys are always welcome here you know that. If we're having to go through this, at least we're all experiencing it together."

We watched them from the front door as they walked out past our cars to get to theirs. But they suddenly stopped and turned back around to face us at the front door. They motioned for us to come out there, so we walked out to see what the problem was. There on my truck, were scratches all the way from the hood to the back bumper on the driver's side.

"Dammit, really, my truck?" I said angrily.

My truck was an older model and one that I used for hauling farm equipment and what not. None of this plastic and aluminum stuff the newer models are made of. It was a battle ax and I've had it for years.

Connie rubbed my back. "I'm so sorry, I know you love that truck. Luckily, if there is a luckily here, it's only scratches and nothing worse."

She always had a positive side, but I was not in the mood for that right then. I was mad. I didn't care if it was only minor damage. The fact that there was any damage was enough. That finding did make sense though. My truck was sitting on the side of the house we heard that loud sound from. But what magnified the sound so much from inside our house? It was like nails down a chalkboard. I would think that it scratching my truck wouldn't have made that much of a sound that we could hear it. Nonetheless, it was an answer but an answer that brought on even more questions.

After seeing what happened to that bobcat, Connie and I got straight to work beefing up or animal's housing. I can't say for sure that the dog man was responsible, we're in the woods, anything could've done that. But we wanted to make sure whatever did that to the bobcat didn't have the chance to do that to our livestock. Our property was all coming together, and the day came for the cows chickens, and pigs to be delivered. John and Marie had come over to help us get everything into place. Seeing as how we were sharing land with some cryptid devil, for the time being, hunting would be limited, at least on our land. John had given Connie and I permission to hunt on his property so that's what we did.

For some reason, the brunt of the incidences were happing at our place. We still had to figure out why. That's where the pigs come into play. If John and Marie have no children, no dogs, and just cows and chickens but were having no activity, to catch this dog man, we're going to have to throw in something to really entice it. This thing toys with you. I know that at any point, it's large enough and strong enough to attack us at any minute, yet it doesn't. The only thing that clicks when we talk about it, is that this is where it has its home, assuming it has a home. It sees this as its territory primarily and Connie and I are living right in the heart of it.

We all sat around the table at John and Marie's and came up with a plan, or, as much of one we could make.

"I don't at all feel its other worldly or paranormal by any means," John said. "I've started doing research on them and they're every-where. I have listened to encounter after encounter, and they all match up for the most part. The one thing that is common in every story I have heard, is that they're just like any other living and breathing animal. They all need shelter, food, and water. On your property, it has all of that. You guys experienced it at the water that day. There alone, it has two things it needs, food and water. You know you have deer and other small game there as well."

Connie smiled a devious smile. "We just need to find out where it lays its head."

"I have some animal calls that I use to hunt," I said. "Why don't we use those to call it in, that's going to get it in quicker."

"Right, I'm sure it will," Marie spoke up, "But it still isn't going to help you locate where it dens up. You'll be drawing it out, but that won't help in the long run."

"I don't know, Marie, maybe since these dogmen come out during the day as well, we can distract it. We can have one of us at the wood line at their house and then one person here making calls. If this dog man is primarily canine and an apex predator, the hearing this thing has, has got to be top notch. If someone is here in our cornfield making animal calls, it will be safe for the other person to go in looking for some sort of cave or large hole or something it has to be using to sleep." John said.

"I guess," Marie said hesitantly, "But is that actually safe?"

Me and John made eye contact at that point. We knew that this would be dangerous, and someone could get hurt. But we didn't want to share that with Connie and Marie. Connie had the mind of a hunter. Her goal was to take down whatever it is no matter what. But would she be willing to sacrifice me or John in the process? No, she wouldn't. But he and I both knew that this would be our best shot at taking care of this problem. Well, we hoped anyway.

"To make this easier, I have several walkie talkies we can use to communicate. Since John knows these woods better than Connie and me, he can be the one to go in and do the search while I hide in the cornfield and make an injured animal call. When I hear something coming in my direction, I will radio him to let it know it's okay for him to go in."

"I don't know guys," Marie went on, "This is just too much. I can't even believe we're sitting here formulating a plan to down something like this. I just feel like we're putting too much at risk."

John reached over and grabbed her hand. "Look, we've hunted all our lives. They've already struck this things curiosity even more so by bringing in pigs. Probably something that's never been there before. That's going to keep it on its toes. I wouldn't agree to this if it were something that wasn't necessary, but wouldn't you want something done so you wouldn't always have to worry about your home, the lives of your animals, and most importantly the safety of you and your loved one?"

"I guess you're right," she conceded, "Just be safe, John. That's all I ask. If you feel you're getting in to deep, get out of those woods."

John smiled, "Deal."

The next couple weeks, Connie and I observed all our animals closely. Something was definitely stirring them up. They always acted different when a predator was around so we would pinpoint the exact times this happened every day to get a handle on when to put our plan into action. Luckily, nothing had been able to get them. Again, the mindset of how this things toys with you. Connie and I had set up motion detectors out back to also ward anything off and to add another layer of protection. Bright halogen lights would come on with any movement from the wood line. The first time they went off, we ran to the window at the back of the house to hopefully see what it was. Nothing but a dang racoon. It just showed us how sensitive the lights were as well as show us how much light they give off.

We all met at John and Marie's early and went over what we had observed. We explained to them that the only thing that tripped our motion detectors were small animals at night when it was completely dark. All our livestock got real worked up however, as soon as dusk came, I'd say around five or a little after.

"With it being daylight longer, it plays in our favor because that doesn't put John in the woods alone at night." Connie said.

We looked like infantry men getting ready for battle. I had my hunting gear on, my rifle on my back, and my walkie talkie in hand. I had grabbed my injured deer call on the way out the door. John met me outside and I found that he too was dressed for war. It almost felt like we were kids again trying to ambush the neighborhood bullies.

Honestly though, I was still having a hard time wrapping my mind around all of this. I could only go off the words of my dear wife and our friends as to what we were even dealing with. I still hadn't fully laid eyes on it. A part of me wanted to while a part of me didn't based on everyone's description and hearing how it affected other people. I certainly didn't want to have a fear of the woods, it was my life.

"The entrance to the woods is about two miles from our house, John. It's five miles from our house to yours. Based on the size of this however, I don't think it would take it long to get from here to there. I will walkie you when I'm in position in the cornfield as well as when I make my first call. I'm not sure if you'll be able to hear it from where you're at or not so we'll just keep that open line of communication so we're all on the same page." I told him.

Just then, Connie queued up her walkie, "Are you guys ready to do this?"

"As ready as we'll ever be, Connie." I said back to her.

Her and Marie were inside keeping an eye out the back window hoping to see it tear through the woods along the wood line to give us a heads up and to let John know when to go in.

"You are going to have to be quick, Mark." Connie said the night before while going back over the plan. "This has speed like you wouldn't believe. Once it hears this call, it should be coming full force and it won't stop. Once I signal you, you must be able to make it back to your truck in time."

Marie had given John the same speech. I get it through. He and I are facing the same amount of danger. If we're being honest, him more so than me. He's going to look for this things den. Who knows what he will find. I brought some pigs blood from the butcher to spread across a section of the cornfield to hopefully give me enough time to get away and to keep it occupied while I tried to get to John.

With the girls in position inside and John in his truck at the entrance to the woods at the dead end, I made my way to their house. My heart was pounding, and my adrenaline was raging through my system. I started having doubts creep in as I drove. What if this doesn't work? What if this makes the situation at home worse than what it is? Then, my worst fear...What if we have to move to finally get away from this monster? I quickly dismissed them. I also tried to think of everything my grandpa would say if he were here. He would tell me I have to stand up for my family and our home. Remember, these things only show themselves to people they want to see them. No fear, son. Get this son-of a-bitch. I had all I needed then. All my doubts erased, and a new air of confidence instilled. I got to their farm and walkied all of them to let them know I was making my way into position. I grabbed the pig's blood out of the back of the truck and made my way to the front right corner of the cornfield. I was in just far enough to not be seen but not too far in to where I wouldn't be able to find my way out.

I spread the blood around in a circumference about fifty feet from where I would be positioned. Still too close for comfort in my opinion. Nonetheless, it was time.

"Making my first call now." I told everyone.

It was so quiet it was almost deafening at this point. I could hear my heartbeat in my ears. That would play in our favor, however. Most anything should be able to hear this. I cupped the call to my mouth and gave three to four calls each at different intensities. Then, I waited. It seemed like forever sitting in a cornfield, surrounded by blood and nothingness while waiting for a ferocious beast to break through.

"Run, Run, Run," Connie yelled over the walkie, "It's coming, Mark. We just saw it and its quickly headed your way. Please hurry!"

John took that que and ran as fast and as hard as he could into the woods, tearing through briars, and thick brush. He searched for any opening or cave he could. He remembered going through here with his old neighbor. Just over the ridgeline and out of breath, he saw it. A very large cave. This must be it.

"I found it," he yelled into the walkie, still trying to catch his breath, "This has to be it, its huge."

I was running as hard as I had ever run before. I was too winded to reply to John and I was hoping either Connie or Marie would answer. My lungs burned with every breath I took, and fear was beginning to overtake me. I could feel tears welling up in my eyes and that's when I heard it. A low, long growl approaching. I had almost made it out of the cornfield, I was home free. Then I fell with a hard thud, and I dropped my walkie. This thing was inching further into the corn. I could hear it's thrashing. No doubt it's found the blood by now. I didn't have time to look for my walkie at that point. I scrambled up as fast I could and made a bee line for my truck. I threw it in reverse, spinning gravel and making a large dust cloud and I hauled ass out of there.

"Mark, come in, are you out of there yet?" Connie pleaded into her walkie. Radio silence.

Marie was pacing the floor and praying. "I knew this was a bad idea, I just knew it."

Connie paid her no mind. "Mark, answer me, are you ok?"

John could hear everything that was going on and tried to reach Mark as well. Just then, John saw movement in the cave. "There's more than one!" he exclaimed. He immediately walkied whoever would listen to him. "Guys, we have a problem there's- "just then, the transmission became garbled and broke up. Silence.

Now both Connie and Marie were frantic.

"John, what's the problem, you broke up, can you repeat?" Connie asked.

"There's more than one of these things," he said fearfully into the mic. "We screwed up, we weren't prepared enough for this."

Connie pleaded into the walkie again, "Mark, please answer me."

I slid into the grass in front of our house and ran inside. I must've looked like a maniac at that point.

"Mark, you're alive!" Connie yelled she threw her arms around my neck and cried.

"Look," I said. "I love you too, but I have to get to John. I dropped my walkie in the cornfield when I fell. Where is John, have you heard from him?" I was spitting out questions left and right. My adrenaline was at an all-time high and I just wanted to get to my friend.

Connie's face changed in an instant. "He found the cave of the dogmen, but there's a problem, a big one." She said.

"What do you mean a problem?" I asked almost frantic.

Suddenly, a noise crackled out of the walkie. "If you can still hear me, I'm hunkering down up here. They spotted me. I could really use some help up here, has anyone heard from Mark yet?"

I grabbed the walkie from Connie. "I'm here buddy where are you at?"

"Mark, thank God you're okay, it's a big cave but there's more than one, I need your help." He said.

"I'm coming but you have to tell me where, John, where are you?"

"I'm at the top of the ridge"- his walkie had gone out again.

I queued up my walkie again. "At the top of what, John you cut out."

"They're coming, the ridgeline, hurry." Then his transmission went silent.

John was lying on his stomach, almost afraid to peer over the large mound of dirt he was hiding behind. Once he gathered enough courage, he pulled out his binoculars and he could clearly see over to their den. They held their noses in the air, and he knew they were trying to sniff him out. Their massive size made them easy to see and he still couldn't believe what it was he was seeing. How is this real? How did they get here? Where did they come from? It was almost as if he were looking at a science experiment gone horribly wrong. An average wolf filled with demons and then they somehow escaped the lab. A genetic mistake and here he was looking at them.

He knew that there wasn't any way a lab could create something like this, however. These creatures were straight from the depths of hell. They were all standing on their back legs walking as if they're human. The fur was long on some but short on the others. Their chests were broad, they had long torsos, and hands instead of paws, except their feet. He noted that their feet were like that of actual dogs.

They didn't all look the same though. Some reminded him of hyenas, and some were just like the werewolves he had seen in movies as a kid. Large protruding snouts with jaws that opened displaying razor sharp fangs that would strike fear into anyone. This creature he was looking at, was pure evil. He had thought back to all the encounters he had listened to and was completely understanding of why people never wanted to go back into the woods after seeing it. He wondered to himself if he ever would after this. After all, he and Marie had animals to harvest for food. He didn't need to hunt at all.

"Marie," his thoughts went to his dear sweet wife at that moment. "I must survive for Marie. She is my whole world and me losing this battle against these hell beasts is not an option."

He turned from his position to look down below him. He hadn't heard anything creeping up on him but with these things, anything is possible. Why couldn't it have been bigfoot, why did it have to be dog man inhabiting these woods? He turned the volume down on his walkie so anything coming through didn't alert them to where he was at. Although, he knew they already did, and they were just messing with him.

"John, come in buddy, please tell me where you are again," Mark said over the walkie. "I need to know exactly where you are so I can come help you."

John fumbled with his walkie. Even the slightest sound at that moment was too loud.

"I'm right at the ridgeline, near the water. I'm hunkered down behind a large mound of dirt. I can see them, Mark. The sun is starting to set, and I need to get the hell out of here." John whispered into the walkie. "They know I'm here. There's no way they can't."

"I'm headed your way now, bud. Don't move unless it's an emergency. We can't risk you getting turned around and then lost in these woods. That would be a fatal mistake." John replied.

I looked at Connie and Marie. They were both like fragile children standing in the kitchen, both on the verge of tears.

"I am taking this walkie with me so I'm going to need you both to trust me. I must be able to communicate with John but that means I won't be able to communicate with either of you. I am going to go get John out of there before it gets any darker. Once complete nightfall comes, he and I are both going to be sitting ducks. The good news is that he didn't have to go too far in before he found them."

Connie walked over to me and hugged me sobbing. "I love you,

Mark, with every fiber of my being. Please come back home to us safely with John.

I pulled away and smiled at her. "I'll do my level best, you know that."

Marie stood silent, not saying a word. She didn't have to. At that point, it was a make-or-break situation. I knew that I had to get John as well as myself, back in one piece.

I ran to my truck and sped as fast as I could. I saw John's truck and I parked off to the side a way behind him and ran the rest of the way in.

"John, come in, I just made it into the woods," I said. "Are you still at the ridgeline?"

"They're making their way into the woods now, Mark. They're all dispersing in different directions."

The sun was setting further behind the horizon, and I knew I had to get to him quick. I started to make my way up to the water where he was at. I could hear far off noises, and I knew based off what he had just told me that it had to be the echoes of the dogmen walking. I saw John in the distance, and I mustered all the strength I had left in my legs to run up to him.

"Come on, we have to get out of here," I said breathlessly as I grabbed his shoulders to pull him to his feet. "I hear them walking and they're bound to be getting closer to us."

As John stood up, his pack got stuck onto a large branch. As he turned around to remove it from the limb, the head of a dog man came up over the mound of dirt. He and I were face to face with one of these hell beasts. Its head was large, and ears pointed. Dark sinister red eyes bore a hole into our souls. Saliva dripped from this thing's fangs and blood covered the dark black fur on its face from what they could only assume to be a recent kill. We were both frozen in fear. What the hell do we do now?

If we turn our backs, we're done for. If we stay here, we face the same fate. John was staggered just enough from me that I felt comfortable pulling my weapon. I slowly pulled my shotgun as this thing snarled and growled at every move I made. My mouth was dry, and my heart was in my throat. I didn't know if me shooting it would do any good, but at this point, it was our only hope.

I would at least injure the damn thing. I said a prayer under my breath, quickly pulled up my gun the rest of the way and fired. My shot was a direct hit right into the face of this dogman. It instantly fell backwards, and we could no longer see it. Not knowing if a shotgun to the face would actually kill one of these creatures, we immediately took off running as fast as we could down the mountain and to our trucks.

Even though our ears were ringing from the shotgun blast, we heard them all clamoring behind us. The echo from the gun hadn't in fact scared them off as I'd hoped. It's almost as if it called them in and they were coming in fast. We raced to the water sliding across the slick rocks as we crossed, and we both fell with a splash. We quickly got to our feet and made our way closer and closer to the exit of the woods. John flew into his truck and I into mine. We started them at the same time and as our bright headlights turned on, we saw them.

4

Their eyes shined brighter than the moon and their large, ghastly figures, outlined the trees. But they didn't come after us. For whatever reason, they stopped almost as if something were keeping them in the woods. We didn't stick around to find out and we raced backwards all the way back to the house.

That way we could keep an eye on them just in case they came after us again. John and I slammed our trucks into park and quickly made our way inside. Connie and Marie both gasped as we came in. I'm sure we looked rough but based on our ordeal, I'm just glad we made it back at all.

They helped us take off our wet clothes that was covered in more than just water if I'm being honest. We both had blood on our faces from the shot that dog man took. The only thing we knew to do then, was pace the floor. We were too filled with adrenaline to sit down, calm down, or do anything. We recounted everything to Connie and Marie as best as we could. But we knew it was all coming out too quickly for them to understand.

"We looked death right in the face tonight," John said shaking. "I don't know if I'll ever go into the woods again knowing those things are in there. Hell, after that we may even move. I know I've seen them in the woods before however, I hadn't ever seen more than what I thought to be one and never that close. I feel bad for not leaving beforehand knowing what I do now."

Marie gasped. "Maybe moving should be a decision that's made when cooler head prevail, John."

He took a deep, ragged breath. "When cooler heads prevail, Marie?" John asked harshly. "I was face to face with one of these damn monsters. Its breath was a stench you can't describe. Its eyes were red and the teeth...the teeth." John couldn't go any further. He broke down then. Marie sat him down and held him as he cried.

I knew then that this was something that would take John a while to get over and he was right, after seeing them that close in the woods, maybe we should all move.

"It really was something of nightmares that we were face to face with guys, you really don't understand. You two have seen it from a distance. We were inches from this thing. There were at least five of them in the woods, six counting the one I shot. But something strange happened as we were leaving, something I found peculiar. When we turned on our lights and started backing up, they didn't come running after us as we expected. It was almost as if they couldn't break some imaginary barrier."

John pulled himself together and apologized for breaking down. I knew it was hard for him, but I understand.

"There's no need to apologize John," Connie said. "But when you two are up to it, we really need to all collectively sit down so you can calmly tell us what it was that was seen. Then, we can regroup and try and figure out what to do from here. Obviously, none of us want to move so we have to figure out how to handle this bunch, if you shooting that one did any good, and where to go from there."

John stood up from the couch and started pacing again. "I need to go home; I want to go home. I would love to take a shower and get all this blood off me."

I stood up and walked over to him and placed my hands on his shoulders. "We'll get through this, bud. I know it's rough right now, but you're not alone. I was there too, and we'll talk it through. How about me and Connie follow you guys' home to make you sure you both get there and inside safely?"

He looked eye to eye with me. "That would be nice. I'm angry and scared right now and I just need to be in my own element. Don't take offence to me wanting to leave. Home is just where I feel the safest."

Connie walked to where we were stood. "It's also further from the woods than where you are now. So, do you guys know if you were able to kill that thing or not?"

"I mean, I shot it in the face, we're covered in the remnants of it. But who knows if I was able to kill it or not. We surely didn't stick around to find out. I know hindsight is always twenty, twenty but if you were in that position, you wouldn't have stayed either. We hauled freight after I shot it and wasn't about to turn around to see if it were dead or not." I said.

"Blood," John said out of the blue recounting things going through his mind, "Its face had blood on it. I could only assume at the time that it was blood from a recent kill but what is the likelihood that this was the one that came through the cornfield, Mark?"

I thought about that for a while. I had poured all that pigs blood in the corn; about two gallons of it. If it were the same beast that ravaged the cornfield, that would explain all the blood on its fur. The thought of that made recalling the encounter even scarier, however.

"If that's true," I exclaimed, "Then that would mean it was the one chasing me through the tall stalks of corn!"

I was relieved I hadn't stop to look for my walkie then. If I would've met that creature in the corn, I am sure that I wouldn't be here now. We only saw the head and a portion of the neck out in the woods but in an instant, that dog man could have been on us and if its head were that large, its body had to have been massive.

"The corn," Marie said with wide eyes and fear coursing through her veins. "There's still all that blood in the cornfield, what if they come back to it knowing it's there?"

"We'll make sure you get in safely, Marie," Connie said. "More than likely, if this were the same dog man that was in the corn, I don't think the others would venture this far. We've all only seen one that matches the description of the one Mark shot and honestly, who is to say that it was the only dog man to come out. We don't know anything about them so it's hard to say."

"Yes, I saw the other ones through my binoculars, and they didn't appear to have anything on them, not like this one did. Come to think of it I never saw it, the one Mark shot. My thought is, now that I think about it further, is that one had to have been in the corn because it wasn't at the den with the rest when I looked. Therefore, it would make sense as to why it wasn't there." John interjected.

"It's a miracle we made it back," I said. "It could have gotten you or me at any given time."

Marie tried to shake that thought from her mind. "We just need to get home, it's already dark which limits our sight but these things I know can see even better at night."

I grabbed my shotgun and watched as John and Marie got in their truck and Connie into ours and we followed them home. Connie kept an eye out to the sides for any movement. I was hoping one didn't decide to jump in front of my truck again. We made it to John and Marie's without incident, we both got out and made sure they got inside safely.

"Please let me know when you get home." They both said. "There's no one to protect you guys."

I smiled at her and John. I knew we would be okay. Having faced what could have been the leader of the pack, then shooting it, left me feeling more confident about things along with trying to figure these dogmen out. I still didn't know exactly what they were so to speak, but if they can be injured, then they can be killed.

We sat at the table the next morning over breakfast and coffee talking of the previous night's events. I was just thankful to still be here to be able to sit with my wife. It could have ended horribly. We stood the possibility of being injured or worse yet, killed by one of these dogmen. That's what I struggled the most with. Not that I wanted to be maimed or killed, but why it didn't attack us when it could have. At some point, I also knew that I would have to back into those woods. I didn't want to put Connie at risk, but I also didn't think

John would be up for a trek into those woods anytime soon, or ever again. To get to the bottom of this whole thing though, someone would have to.

What I was anxious to see, is if that dog man was dead lying just over that large mound of dirt. It should be, given the shot it took to the face. But I knew getting Connie on board with this wouldn't be easy.

We waited until mid afternoon to go out and make sure all our livestock had what they needed. We decided to get them on a different schedule and started giving them more food at night. We didn't want to be out in the early morning hours just in case. I decided now was a better time than any to drop my plan onto Connie.

"You're joking right, Mark. Good one, but that's not happening." She said as tossed grains and corn to the chickens.

"Connie, do we ever leave a dead or injured animal in the woods that we've shot?" I was hoping if I used hunting, she wouldn't be able to disputer it.

"Well, no of course not, Mark." She said as she turned to face me.

"Ok, so this isn't any different," I said trying hard to get her to go along with it. "It's somewhat of an animal and we need to go see if it can be killed. If it can, we're home free. That means they all can."

Connie thought it over. "Well, this is different. This dog man isn't your typical animal that you hunt in the woods. If it isn't dead, it will be looking for revenge and extremely pissed off because you tried to blow it's face off."

She wasn't wrong but at the same time, we had to know to be able to move any further or plan anything at all.

"Well, I guess I'll go out on my own then." I said as I walked away.

I heard the shovel she was holding in her hand hit the ground hard and I turned around.

"Fine, Mark," she said angrily. "I will go to the woods with you but on one condition. We have to let Marie and John know we're going because if something happens to us out there, someone has to know where we went."

I knew what we were planning on doing wouldn't be something

that either of them would go for. Walking into their living room the next day, I was as nervous as a long-tailed cat in a room full of rocking chairs.

"You're not serious, you guys." Marie said.

John just hung his head. "Mark, Connie, please. Do not go back into those woods."

I knew what they were thinking and if I were in their shoes, I would have been saying the same things. I probably would've been a little harsher. But that wasn't their nature. We explained to them why and they understood but still didn't like the idea.

"Well, how are going to know something has happened to you. We can't just let you run in the woods without a way to communicate." Marie said anxiously.

"I have three walkie talkies," I told them, "The fourth is in your cornfield."

"That's right, John said, "I forgot about that."

I had a thought just then. "Let's see what the condition of your corn is, maybe we will find the walkie on the way. I know I dropped it right at the edge of the corn so it's not like it's in the thick part."

John chuckled. "Did you hit your head on a rock the other night when you fell in the water? You really want me to go into my cornfield that's covered in pig's blood to look for a walkie?

I'll admit, not the smartest. But at the same time, I was curious. I wondered if this beast came out this way after me or went another way.

"We all know they're here, that's no question but we have to know what makes them tick, if they can be injured, if they can be killed, and why didn't they come after us that night." I said pleading my case.

Connie was just looking at me. I could tell her wheels were spinning. I was hoping she would say something. She stood up then and walked to their screened front door. Silence. She finally turned to face us.

"I know he sounds like he's lost his mind and I too thought the same when he told me what he wanted to do. But the fact of the matter is, is he's right. It's just us out here. No one would ever in a million years believe what happened. We only have each other. If we don't go out to see if this dogman, he shot the other night is dead, we'll never know how to truly defeat them or if they even can be defeated. Then all of us, will have to either live in fear or pick up and move. I don't see where we have any other choice." Connie said adamantly.

Thank God, she's on my side. I can't do any of this alone. Something of this magnitude must be done together; either the two of us or the four of us. Connie walked outside with me to go look for my walkie. I remember the last time I was here. I was running for my life with a literal hell hound on my trail. I didn't think I would make it to my truck. I imagined it lunging on me from behind, pulling me to the ground, and tearing me to pieces. The worst part of that feeling, is that no one would ever know until they came back. I shook the thought from my head, thankful that worst case scenario never played out. Then I heard Connie yell for me. She had walked a little way ahead of me. Not too far to where I couldn't see her.

I ran over to her as she knelt and picked up what was left of my walkie. It was in pieces. She picked up the largest handheld part and the cover fell off pulling the wires inside out with it. Smaller pieces of plastic littered the ground. This didn't appear to have any teeth marks though. Which means this was stomped on. I tried to think back to when I fell. Did I fall on it or step on it? I couldn't have, this was on my side. If I had crushed it, it would have had to be in the front because I fell on my face. For me to step on it, I would have had to have backtracked. I didn't. I also wasn't heavy enough to do this much damage. These walkies were sturdy. They weren't some cheap plastic walkie talkies that breaks or quits working after a few days. That means it did run this way, it was behind me hunting me.

"This dog man is heavy without question," I said to Connie. "It was chasing me and followed me this way. My truck was right over there almost where we're parked now."

"Man, Mark, that's not far at all. I'm glad you're a fast runner." She said looking over at me.

Connie and I made our way back to the house and showed John

and Marie what was left of the walkie. John took it from me and looked it over all the while, shaking his head.

"Well," John said smiling, "I guess we need to work out a plan."

Marie scoffed and shook her head.

Connie and I looked at each other confused but eager to hear what he had to say.

"You can each take a walkie in case the two of you get separated and then me and Marie will have the third."

I don't know what snapped in his brain from being totally against this to now, fully on board with us going back into the woods. I wasn't going to ask either in fear he would change his mind.

We sat down that evening and formulated how things would go, when we would enter the woods, and what all we would take in with us.

The next evening, John and Marie showed up at our house. They were going to stay there, armed to the teeth while Connie and I made it into the woods. Geared up and ready to go, we came up with a code word to yell over the walkie just in case things went south for both Connie and me. We decided to go with the traffic light system. Code red meaning to stop, code yellow meaning proceed with caution, or code green meaning it's safe to go or come in.

We drove to the edge of the woods and just sat there for a minute taking in how ominous they now looked. I envisioned all the dogmen almost reaching for us but not coming out. That part still got me. What was keeping them in the woods? We got out and cautiously looked all around us. We had each other's backs and safety was number one. If Connie was facing forwards, I was looking behind us and vice versa. We made it to the water's edge. Not one single sound could be heard. The water sounded so loud against the silent back-drop of the forest. It's almost like everything there knew that there was a predator around. I was second guessing this now. Maybe they were right, maybe we shouldn't have come. But it's too late for that now, we're here and we have no choice. This is our home.

We moved ahead slowly, weapons drawn and ready. A little further up from the water, sat the large mound of dirt. There was still dried blood all over the ground and it was covered in small flies. I stood staring at the vast open space where the dogman's head once filled. I remembered feeling it's hot breath, its glowing red eyes, and its sharp fangs. The growl is something you'll never forget though.

Connie reached over and touched my arm. "Are you ok doing this, Mark?"

In reality, no. I wasn't at all. All I had to do was look over that dirt mound to hopefully find the remains of something that shouldn't exist. I just couldn't make my body move from its place.

"Do you want me to look?" Connie asked noticing fear in my eyes.

I sighed. "No, this is something I must do. I had the guts to shoot it. I have to have the guts to look and see if it's dead."

Fear pricked every hair on my body to stand on end. I was afraid if I looked over, that another one would pop up again just as it had that night. But this time, I don't think I would be as lucky. I finally got both my head and my legs in tune with one another and walked forward. I got down on my knees, took a ragged breath, and peered over the side. I turned around and Connie had inched closer to me with her shotgun ready to fire.

"It's-It's-gone...I was finally able to get my words out.

Connie looked at me in amazement. "I thought you said you shot it in the face, how is it gone?"

I was just as confused. It shouldn't have survived that; nothing would survive that.

The sun almost instantly went down at that point. Eerily enough, a band of fog followed the darkness. Off in the distance, thunder rolled across the sky and a howl could be heard. It was almost like it was calling attention to the others that we were here.

Connie looked at me "This is like some horror movie, Mark, I don't know if this was such a good idea."

"I know, but we're here now. That dog man is gone, and I don't know how. It's not going to have any face at all," I said. "Let's go a little further in and see what we find. I don't hear anything now, just thunder, we'll look a bit more and leave before the rain comes."

I could tell she didn't agree with me, but she went along with it anyway. The thunder cracked louder overhead. Lightning then began illuminating the woods.

"The further in we go, the worse this is getting. I think we should leave now." Connie said beginning to turn around.

I turned to follow her. I pulled out my flashlight and that's when I saw it. A foot print. An actual human footprint. But this wasn't normal. Who has a print that big?

Connie turned when she heard me abruptly stop. Our eyes met and she knew something was up. I held my finger to my mouth for her to be quiet and I shone my flashlight on the print. Her eyes grew wide with fear.

"Bigfoot." I said in amazement. "Bigfoot are also here."

5

Connie put her head in her hands, obviously flustered. I knew she was nearing her breaking point. But the facts were right in front of us. There's nothing else that could've made that print.

"You're kidding me," Connie groaned. "Where the heck did we move to, Mark, some cryptid jungle?"

I cued up my walkie. "John, you guys are never going to believe what we've found here. Connie and I are ten-four. We'll fill you in when we get back. We're headed out now. Rains moving in."

"How about the dog man, Mark, can you at least tell me that before you get here?" John asked.

"Gone," I said. "That thing isn't there."

We made it out of the woods without incident. I was hoping that these dog men would give us a break seeing as how they knew we would kill them or try to at least. We loaded up in the truck and headed back. John and Marie were sitting in the kitchen at the table when we made our way inside. We both joined them at the table.

"Did we imagine it, Mark, was this some mass hallucination between the two of us?" John asked perplexed.

"I don't know, John. I clearly shot it right in the face. Nothing could survive a shot like that but I'm here to tell you, that dog man was not where it should've been."

"There's more than enough blood on the ground to indicate that what you two experienced really happened. You two witnessed something that night and were both part of successfully shooting it. There were flies on the blood and everything you would expect, just no body." Connie said.

John leaned back in his chair and met eyes with Marie. I could tell they were thinking what Connie and I had thought while we were in the woods. If this thing survived that shot, we're screwed.

"So, what else did you find," Marie asked. "You said we weren't going to believe it."

"Bigfoot," I blurted out, "We were getting ready to leave and I turned my flashlight on and that's when I saw the print next to the water. I could only assume it was wading through and left that deep impression when it made its way to the other side."

John carried the same look on his face that Connie had in the woods. Marie sat silent, mouth wide open in shock.

"You know, I wonder if that's what we saw the first time we went in the woods. We thought it was a bear, maybe it was a Bigfoot. Then, when we were near the water, and smelled that awful smell, could that have been a bigfoot as well" Connie asked.

I sat and thought about that and couldn't help but lean towards agreeing with her. Granted, the dog-man's breath was wretched, but we didn't really smell anything else. Of course, we also hadn't paid any attention to anything at that moment except for our own survival. Maybe it was a bigfoot we smelled. I thought back to what my grandpa had told me about them. Some people who encountered them claimed to have smelled a foul odor but then some didn't.

"Are you telling me that we not only have dogmen in the woods, but we now also have Bigfoot, are you sure it wasn't a bear that just double stepped?" John asked me.

"That's exactly what I'm telling you and I can, with about one hundred percent certainty, tell you it wasn't a double step of a bear.

Connie and I have seen that before and that print was nothing like the one we just came across."

It only meant one thing. We would have to go back into the woods to sort this out. The good thing is that three of the four of us were okay with it. Marie wasn't. I don't know if she ever would be. She was traumatized. I'm not too sure how she felt about bigfoot, however. But nonetheless, it didn't hold any weight to the facts that had played out in front of us.

"This is a lot guys," Marie said, "Do you think we should bring someone else in to do the investigations. I think we're in over our heads here. I thought we were from the beginning in dealing with dog man, but now there's a bigfoot too."

If there was one thing that held conflict between John and Marie, this would've been it. I could see John's frustration with her when it came to this subject. I could only assume that he wished Marie had the same confidence as Connie. But I could also see Marie's side. It was a catch twenty-two of which there would be no winner, only compromise.

"Absolutely not," John said. "I don't want strangers coming up here on our property just as I'm sure they don't either. They'll want to interview us, they'll be all over our land, and they haven't been here since day one. We would have to explain everything to them repeatedly. All three of us are trained hunters. If we can survive an attack from this, then we can handle a bigfoot."

I looked over at Marie. "I think researchers mean well and they do find interesting evidence. But they'll be coming here to look for what we have already found. We don't need evidence of their existence; we need a solution to the fact that they exist here at all. From what I learned as a young kid, bigfoot are generally harmless unless threatened."

"What do you think the connection is between dogmen and bigfoot," Connie asked. "Did your grandpa ever say anything about that?"

I chuckled. "No, grandpa didn't say anything about dogmen. Of course, back then, they could've gone by a different name. Maybe they just called them werewolves back in those days. I'm not certain what the correlation could be between the two, honestly. I would think it would be a clash for territory. But one thing is certain, they're both here on our property. I knew we would have to take a different approach to this to fully understand what was going on and how to handle it.

"John, I think a good approach to begin with, is to pull any website you searched a couple weeks ago and see if they're have been any reports made for our area or surrounding areas for either dog man or bigfoot. Did you or your neighbor ever experience anything strange outside of the visual you two had?" I asked.

John thought about that. "Well, no. But I also don't really know the signs to look for concerning bigfoot. We just had those two visuals of this creature. I guess there could've been signs all around us but not knowing what to look for, or even considering that a bigfoot could've been here, we didn't pay attention."

Connie spoke up. "What would the likelihood be that maybe this, what we call dogman, is some misidentified bigfoot?

I didn't know if that could be possible. What John and I saw in the woods was nothing at all like what my grandpa had described. His encounters were with something large, broad, and had similarities of apes. What we saw was clearly canine. Long snout, sharp teeth, and pointed ears. Nothing at all fitting the description I had heard of bigfoot. Of course, it is all up for interpretation. Maybe some people have seen dogmen and thought they were bigfoot. There are so many unknowns, it was just hard to tell.

"How about me and Marie head home and I'll see what I can come up with," John said, "In the meantime, you and Connie stay put and out of those woods. I appreciate the spirit you guys have of solving this, but it has to be done together. It also has to be handled carefully so none of us get hurt. It's not worth risking our lives over."

Connie and I laid in bed that night trying to piece everything together. I tried to recount everything that we saw that could be bigfoot sign. Honestly, we were in the same position John was. We weren't paying attention. We would have to go back and look. The storm was bad that night. The wind blew with such force and the rain pounded the roof. Thunder woke me up in the middle of the night with a loud crack. I got up and went to the restroom and walked to the kitchen for a glass of water. I looked out the window facing the back of our property and hoped our animals had gone into their respective homes to get out of the rain.

Lighting flashed and lit up the yard. In that brief instance of light, I saw the shadow of something dart across from left to right. I thought I was just seeing things and hoped for another burst of lightning. Success! This time it was headed back the way it came but it looked like it was carrying something. An awful thought instantly came to mind. Our animals! This thing just took one of our chickens!

I ran to our bedroom. "Connie, wake up! This thing just took one of our chickens, we have to go secure the coop now!

Thunder roared overhead again. Connie sprung from the bed and threw on her rain boots and raincoat. It was absolutely pouring. The rain fell so hard, we could hardly hear each other talk.

"There's a hole in the top of the coop, Mark, this is metal netting, how did they get in here?" Connie yelled over the thunder crashing.

"What about the chicken house itself, it's wooden. The chicken would've been in there because of the rain." I yelled back.

Connie looked closer. "No Mark, there's no damage to the chicken house. It's like whatever this was just reached in and grabbed it. We need to at least get a tarp to throw over the top to block the rain and we'll come back in the morning and look when we can see better and hopefully then, it's not raining."

I ran to the garage and got our big blue tarp and some zip ties. We secured the coop as much as possible and went back inside. Connie was angry. She threw her yellow rainslicker into the mudroom along with her boots.

"This is B.S. That is a brutal storm, Mark, what would even trek out into that to steal a chicken? Are you sure it was just one?" Connie asked as she dried herself with a towel.

"I can only assume it was one," I said. "I was standing at the sink looking out the window when lightning lit up the yard. I saw a large, dark shadow run from left to right and then when lightning flashed again, it was running from right to left and this time, with a chicken. That's when I ran and woke you up."

Connie glanced at her watch and realized it was almost five o'clock in the morning. "No sense in trying to go back to bed after that. Would you like some coffee?" she asked as she made her way to the kitchen.

I finished drying off and walked to the kitchen with her. "Yes, I'd love some. Thank you."

I called John a little after eight. I explained to him what happened. Connie and I had already been out to check the coop and all the other animals. It looked like only that one chicken was taken but that was still one too many.

"Have you been able to find anything out," I asked. "Nothing had gone near our livestock until last night. I don't believe in coincidences, but this is a little strange that nothing happened until we spotted that bigfoot print. I don't know if they just showed up on our property or if they've always been here. All I know is that when we thought it was just dog man, as strange as it sounds, nothing messed with them."

"I did right much digging last night when Marie and I got home, and this is what I found. The dog man was first sighted back in the late eighteen hundreds in Michigan. It seems that sightings of this creature start there and go all the way up to today in different locations.

Since we're bringing bigfoot into the mix now, I had to look them up as well. They have a bigger history than this dog man does. But it seems like both cryptids have been widely played into the creature culture. I followed that rabbit trail and found they do in fact go by different names such as bear-wolf, man-wolf, and indigenous dog man. I also read that some people have said it was a type or separate species of bigfoot, but obviously, no one knows for certain. I did however find a picture that had I think seven different pictures of this dog man creature. I can tell you with certainty that I saw two of the seven. The one you shot that we were face to face with, was on the list. I saw another one through my binoculars before you got there that night at the ridgeline, that looked like a hyena, which was also on that list."

To say I was impressed would be an understatement. He had to have been up for a long time pulling all that information.

"Thank you for doing all that, John, I really appreciate it. It's very insightful. Did you happen to see any way that we can safely get rid of them?" I asked.

"I've seen a few ways, but none are fool proof. I read putting bright lights on your property and leaving them on, spreading salt around, and then I read something about putting sulfur around your property. I also read an article about putting trail cameras up. For some reason, trail cameras help deter them both, the bigfoot and the dogmen. But again, I'm not sure if this will deter some and not others or not. It's not like they had an area to where people could leave reviews on what worked and what didn't."

I laughed at that. "No, I get it, I appreciate you looking all that up. I'll get with Connie and maybe we'll leave just leave some bright lights on or put some trail cams up near our animals. At this point, maybe we'll just do both."

He and I hung up the phone and I was telling Connie about everything John had said. We drove to town to the hardware store to get brighter lights than what we had and then we went and got some trail cameras. You can't be too cautious, I guess. We had everything set up and added lights to our whole back lot. That way if anything came out at any direction, it would light up like a football stadium. While we were getting things cleaned up, we heard vehicles coming towards our house. Connie and I both looked at each other. It's not like folks to drive down this way and we weren't expecting John and Marie at all. But sure enough, John's truck was the first vehicle that was seen, then a four door beat up sedan which we had never seen before. I know John wouldn't bring a stranger to our home without good reason so we both walked to the front to figure out what was going on.

"Hey," John said as he got out of the truck and walked to shake my hand. "I tried to call both your house and your cell phone, but you didn't answer. I wanted to introduce you to someone that can help us."

To be honest, I was a little perturbed. We had talked about not bringing outsiders into this. Now, here he was with someone who can "help" us. I was cordial; however, it wasn't his fault.

"My name is Mark, and this is my wife Connie," I said walking up to shake his hand.

He didn't appear threatening or like he was just going to waltz in here and try to take over. He was taller, younger than all of us, tanned skin, dark hair, pleasant attitude.

"It's a pleasure to meet you both," he said. "I used to live here. My name is Ashton Samuels. I lived here with my wife and our children."

Wow, if we could have used anyone's knowledge concerning this creature and our portion of the woods, his was it. He could give us so much insight on everything, like when the activity started for them, how long it was until this creature started harassing them, and more importantly, did he also experience the bigfoot that was here. See, when we purchased the house from them, it was strictly between us and the realtor. We signed all our documents online and sent them over and at closing, our schedules never matched up to be there at the same time. So, I hadn't ever met him face to face.

"Yes," I said excitedly, "It's nice to meet you, we've done right much to the place since you were here last. Come on, I'll show you around and we can talk."

We all walked to the back yard and started show him everything we had added, fixed up, and our livestock.

"You're really brave putting all these animals here," Ashton said. "We had our dog and a few chickens but that's it. We were told by the owners before us that bringing any kind of animal here would be a bad idea."

John and I cut our eyes at each other. "I see, did he happen to say why?" I asked curiously.

Ashton shrugged his shoulders. "He didn't really go into detail; said he didn't want to talk about it. But he was peculiar anyway, so I didn't pay it any mind. I wish I would have now. It could've saved my wife and I a lot of heartache and stress."

Just then, he noticed the chicken coop with the large blue tarp over it. He walked over to it and was looking at the ground around the whole perimeter of it. John, myself, and Connie walked over.

"What are you looking for?" Connie asked.

"It was here wasn't it," Ashton said as he looked at us over top of the coop. "That's why the blue tarp is here. I was looking for any prints.

I walked around to the back where he was standing. "What was here?" I asked.

I already knew the answer to the question, but I wanted him to say it almost as confirmation we were talking about the same thing.

"I don't know exactly what "it" was," Ashton said. "I had only seen it once, but it was like nothing I had ever seen before. It was tall, had to have been every bit of seven feet tall or maybe a little more. It had a long torso, and its eyes glowed an amber color. My wife and I saw it coming out of the woods at the dead end one night when we were walking. We saw it coming through the trees. The moon illuminated it just enough for us to get a good look at it. It was almost like a hyena that you see in the wild or at zoos. But I hadn't ever seen a hyena that tall or walk on its hind feet. When it growled, even though it probably wasn't the best idea, we ran."

Connie sighed, "Great." She said in a hushed tone under her breath.

I was curious. If he and his wife had seen it and close enough to give some kind of description, how did they survive that? If they saw it coming out of the woods, why didn't it attack them?

"Are you saying this thing didn't chase you and your wife when you took off running?" John asked confused.

"No sir, it never broke the tree line. I glanced behind me only once to make sure it hadn't come after us. I knew if it did, we wouldn't have made it home. But I saw it standing there growling, mouth wide open and not moving."

This had me baffled. Why are they not coming out? Clearly the one I shot had no problem leaving that area. I had no choice but to dismiss it and I went on and told Ashton what happened with the chicken.

"It didn't stay here and eat it?" He asked, puzzled.

"No, like I said, I saw the shadowed figure carrying it back towards woods," I said, "Is that a strange behavior or something you hadn't seen before?"

Ashton stood silent as he looked at the ground. "Something got our chickens too, but it wasn't carried back to the woods, that to me personally, is strange. I just never put two and two together that what my wife and I saw that night, could've been what got our chickens until now. We just figured it was something else that lived in the woods, you know, something that is of this world. But maybe, it wasn't."

I felt bad for the kid. Reality just smacked him hard in the face. "I'm not saying that what killed your chickens wasn't a natural animal. It absolutely could have been. But if it weren't, in my opinion, I don't think it was the one you and your wife had seen. I think it was one that was more evil and more sinister." I said.

Ashton looked at all of us, eyes racing. "There's more than just that one?" he asked, clearly shaken up. "I just assumed the one we saw that night was the one that tore up the side of our house, almost like it was saying to stay away, a warning if you will."

6

J ohn chuckled, "Oh yes, there's more than one. I personally seen the one you described, but there's more than one of them in the woods over here." he said.

"But we saw that one out in the woods a couple times, John, remember we were hunting and saw it twice." Ashton said.

"I remember it well, Ashton," John said answering, "But if you remember, the one we saw twice was blacker than any black, it didn't look like a hyena."

He stood silent, "You're right John, I guess I just blocked it out. I remember now, I was terrified."

"That's a typical trauma response," Connie said reassuringly. "It's okay.

"Let me ask you a question," I began. "If you don't know the answer, it's okay. There's something else my wife and I discovered and I'm curious if you had seen it, heard it, or possibly smelled it."

I was hesitant to even say the word.

"This may sound outlandish, but it can't be any stranger than what we've already been talking about. Bigfoot, Ashton, did you or your wife ever experience a bigfoot?"

He laughed at that, "Oh, no sir, no bigfoot. I think we would've moved a lot sooner had we seen one of them as well. We moved after our house got torn up on that side. That was just too close for comfort for us with our children being here and them playing in the back. We knew this could be seen out in the daytime when I went hunting with John, but I thought it was something that would stay in the woods. But after it scratched up our house, we found out it wasn't afraid of humans and would get close to the house. We moved shortly after that. Can't have it attacking one or both kids and attacking our dog. Plus, the size of the print I found in the loose dirt by the house, indicated something that had to be massive in size." He paused then, "Wait, have you guys seen a bigfoot on this property?"

We walked back up to the house and sat down in the kitchen. John and I told him about our encounters with this dog man and how Connie and I discovered the bigfoot print when we went back to the woods. It was terrifying to recount but we were trying to get answers.

"You shot that thing in the face, and it didn't die?" Ashton asked shocked.

Connie poured herself another cup of coffee. "Yep, it wasn't lying over the ridgeline where you would think it would be after taking a shot like that. The blood was there, but nothing else."

"That fact that this happened near the water is scary to me," Ashton said taking a drink of his tea. "I took my son there fishing many times. I'm so glad nothing happened to us while we were there."

John and I were thinking the same thing. We would love to try to get him into the woods with us. I wasn't sure how fond of the idea he would be, but it wouldn't hurt to ask.

"Let's cut to the chase," I said sternly. "We have experienced hell right in our face, we know there's more than one of these things and now, there has been sign of bigfoot. John has done research on how to keep these things off our property but what we need to know, is how we can get rid of them all together. I know bigfoot isn't bad like these dogmen are. I was told many a story by my grandpa about bigfoot. But these dogmen though, they have to go. What we learned, is they're the cockroaches of the forest. Now, you're the only around here that we know of, that has had experiences with these things like we have. Would you be willing to go with us into the woods to get a better idea of how to handle this?"

We all sat looking at Ashton waiting for an answer. I felt bad for being so harsh with him, but we had to know. We didn't really have time for anymore small talk. I could tell he was nervous as I sat watching him and to be honest, I would be to. He had a wife, children, a family. He was not obligated to help us in any way, shape, or form. They moved away for a reason. The good thing is, he obviously had some interest in helping or he wouldn't have come back here with John in the first place.

"Cell phones are of no use in the woods, there's no signal," Ashton said out of nowhere. "John said you guys had been using walkie talkies which is smart. We need to set trail cams up as far out as possible. They'll keep them further way from here. I had talked to someone who was knowledgeable in wildlife, not necessarily dog men per se', but they have to have to have some of the same tendencies I would think. They all eat, drink water, and have to have shelter. How far away was the cave from this house, John?"

We were all taken aback by Ashton and his response. He was quiet at first, seemed timid. It was almost like what happened with John, an instant flip of the switch and he was all for having me and Connie go into the woods. The same switch flipped for Ashton right in front of our faces.

"I guess maybe half a mile," John stammered out. "I had my binoculars on to get a good look."

"The prints I saw when I lived here were big, but in no way, were they like bigfoot. They were like wolf prints. I did some of my own research after we moved from here. There is not one good thing about them that I found. Encounters of people going missing, animals, people's pets. I don't think getting rid of them is realistic. I don't think they can be wiped out altogether. The one you shot didn't die, which would suggest maybe like they're something out of this world. Do they come from another dimension? That I don't know, but some of the encounters I have listened to have suggested that. So, getting rid of them is a stretch, but we can try to at least keep them away from this property."

Another dimension? Has this turned into a science fiction novel? Large wolves from another world, walking into ours, wreaking havoc and then leaving again to go back to their dimension. I have to be honest, my mid was spinning. The information John found didn't suggest any of that. It was all factual information that was documented.

"So, I take you will go with us then?" Connie asked since me nor John had said anything else and sat quiet. "We have halogen lights, trail cameras, walkie talkies, we just need another set of eyes. Someone else who knows something about this."

Ashton reached out and shook my wife's hand. "I'll be here, I'll do everything I can to help but, if it gets bad out there, we can't be heroes, we must leave. These creatures are big, strong, and powerful. I know you know that based off your own experience. You won't win one on one with them. I'm glad Mark and John did, but they're obviously the exceptions to the rule. I guarantee it won't happen twice."

Ashton left and went home to talk to his wife about everything. Connie and I finished making sure everything was taken care of on our property. John left as well to go talk to Marie. She was over the whole thing and was just trying to keep away from it as much as possible. She wanted to tuck it away and be done. I understood her stance, though. I wished we could all do that, but this was our reality. To be able to continue living our fairytale life as Marie wanted to see it, we had to take care of the evil villain.

That night, Connie and I made one last check of the property before going inside to get ready for bed. Night had just fallen. Connie had double checked the chicken coop one last time. She walked up to the deck with me, and we sat in the chairs facing our yard. Our porch light was on as bright as it could be. I didn't know if that would keep them away from us or if that would just illuminate us to be easier prey for them. But were tired of not being able to enjoy what we worked so hard for. Being prisoners of the concrete jungle, we came from, we always used to talk of how nice it would be to be able to just sit outside, no neighbors, no noises except those of insects, our own hide away. Now we were fighting for it.

"Do you feel like something, or someone is watching us, Mark?" Connie asked.

I looked around the property as much as I could see. I didn't see or hear anything.

"I think we're just being paranoid, now. If something or someone was around, these lights would come on and we would have plenty of time to get inside. I said trying to reassure her.

Just then, the hair on my arms stood on end. I looked down at them and called Connie's attention to it.

"I think we should go in," she said. "I don't feel comfortable sitting out here anymore."

A low, snarling growl echoed through the woods. In an instant, it sounded like a freight train was coming straight at us through the trees. As soon as it stepped on the property, the lights came on and lit up the whole back area. We saw it then. Tall, blacker than black, with glowing eyes, and a look of pure hatred on its face. We stood up to run when we heard in the distance, a yell that I had only heard my grandpa tell me about. Bigfoot. We watched this thing back up and almost dissolve into the trees. A loud knock followed the yell and then everything fell silent. Not one footstep could be heard. No growling. Nothing. Connie and I looked at each other confused and quickly went inside.

"Was that a bigfoot yelling?" Connie asked me.

"Yes," I said rubbing my face trying to wrap my mind around what just happened. "Not only was that a bigfoot, but that dog man retreated when it heard it. That bigfoot saved our lives!"

"Are you telling me that these ravenous beasts listen to bigfoot now? You don't really expect us to believe that." Marie scoffed as they sat talking over dinner a few nights later.

I'll be the first to admit that this was getting stranger and stranger as time went on, but this was happening, and we had no choice but to go with the hand that was playing out in front of us. I never in a million years would've thought that either so I fully understand where she was coming from.

"I thought for sure that these things could tear anything to shreds it encountered. Maybe that's why they don't leave the wood line, maybe they can't." John said.

"What about the one that would venture over here, though." Connie said. "Was that one exempt from the rules?"

I'm sure there had to be boundaries. If dogmen are somehow controlled by bigfoot as weird as that is, there had to be some understanding.

"In all honesty, have any of us seen this creature outside of the woods? I mean, apart from when I drew it into the corn of course and the time it crossed the road" I said.

They all thought about it.

"Well, no, come to think of it, I haven't," Connie said. "That night I saw it, it was in the behind the trees but still technically in the woods."

John interrupted. It came out that night we were there, and it scratched your truck, and it came out when it tore up the side of yalls house when Ashton and his family lived there too."

"I also think that's the same one I shot, John," I said. "Maybe that one was a rogue one. There has to be one in every group. My grandpa told me one time that when the children of bigfoot grow up, if they're bad so to speak, they cast them out. Then, the bigfoot have to fend for themselves. Maybe it's the same way here with dogmen."

I knew it was all speculation. We didn't know anything about these creatures. I only know what I know about bigfoot because of my grandpa. I had no doubt however, that there are more to those as well than what my grandpa told me.

"So, what do you guys think Ashton's wife will say about what he's planning?" Connie asked.

"I can only assume that she's not going to want him to do it after they dealt with it while they were here, John said "That's the reason they moved to begin with and here he is wanting to go back in the woods."

I knew that that would be a possibility. He could come back here or call John and say that his wife just wasn't going to let him go back in there knowing what she does. I can't say that I blame her after we faced what we did that night in the woods. I hoped not though, we could really use him. Since he lived here and went out with John, he would still know more than Connie and me. Also, seeing as how he had more experiences with this thing, even more so than John, he would be very instrumental in helping us.

"I don't know," Connie said, "He seemed pretty adamant about coming back."

"I guess time will tell, but we need to start restocking all our supplies," I said. "I'm also going to pick up some more walkie talkies. Marie, I know you don't want anything to do with this and I understand. I wouldn't dare ask you to go into those woods with us. But we would still need your help if you're willing to do that for us."

Marie was quiet. I knew she wanted to stay as far away from this thing as possible, but she also wanted to be there for her husband and us as her friends.

"How can I help you guys if I'm not in the woods," Marie finally asked. "Isn't that where most of this stuff is going to happen?"

"Well, not necessarily, Marie," John said "We would have you stay inside at Mark and Connie's house to be a look out. You would have your own walkie talkie for communication and if you happen to see anything at all, you will just let us know. That simple. That keeps you out of harm's way and allows you to be a part of this whole thing. I know deep down you want to help, and I know that right now, your fear for these creatures is controlling you. I get it. They have set up every safety measure they can there now. If anything at all comes onto their property, the whole thing lights up like noon of day. So, what do you say, can you help us by doing that?"

John made it as simple for her as he could. He wanted her to feel included and still give her some kind of control. That would also help with her fear. Before Marie had a chance to answer, John's phone rang. It was Ashton. John put the phone on speaker so we could all listen.

"Hey so, I talked to my wife. She's not entirely going for the whole idea of me going to chase monsters in the woods with my friends. However, she's sympathetic to the position you all are in here. She remembered how she felt when we lived there. I explained everything to her and the background in hunting we all had, that way she knew our chances of survival would be greater than that of a novice hunter going out there. She's agreed to my going along with you guys, but only if she could be there as well. However, she doesn't want to be in the woods where either of these creatures live. Would it be ok if she stayed at Mark and Connie's?"

I jumped on the opportunity. If Marie came along, she wouldn't be alone, and she would be with someone who shared in her opinion about these creatures and how supposedly crazy we are to be going after them.

"Tell her that's fine." I told John.

"You can let her know that I will be there as well," Marie said smiling. She won't just be sitting around an empty house all by herself."

John smiled at Marie and let Ashton know everything would be good to go on all accounts.

"Great," Ashton said. "We will be sending our children to their grandparent's whichever night we come over. You guys just let me a know a day and I'll let you know when we're on the way."

"Well, that takes care of that," Connie said standing from the table. "Come on Marie and I'll help you wash up the dishes."

They both walked to the kitchen and John and I walked outside to the front deck. The sun hadn't quite set yet and we hadn't heard anything around either of the properties since that bigfoot call chased off the dog man.

"How crazy is this whole situation," I asked John. "Did you ever in a million years think that we would become great friends and end up chasing big, bad scary monsters at night through the woods?"

John laughed. "I can't say I did, Mark. Not what I expected the first night we met you and Connie that's for sure."

Monsters or not, I was glad that we had formed this friendship with them. I don't remember ever having a friendship quite like this. We shared a lot of the same commonalities. I think that helped our bond be even stronger. Then you throw in monster hunting, yeah, there's that aspect of the friendship. I had laid in bed one night almost comparing us to the ghostbusters and instead of chasing slimer or the stay puffed marshmallow man, it was dogmen and bigfoot. In situations like this, you have to make the best of it. You can either laugh about it or well, live in fear from it. We may not have proton packs or a ghost trap but, we're going to do the best we can.

"So, we get these trail cams set up as far into the woods as we can, and this is said to keep them away. I think we would at least need ten to twelve of them to put up. Connie and I just went and brought some for our back lot for the animals so we can always use them. If we're keeping these things away from us altogether, we won't need them for our property anymore. That is if they work in keeping them away." I said.

"Yeah, that's the plan anyway. I would also love to know what power bigfoot have over dogmen. I'll have to see if I can drum up more information about that. It all seems so strange to me." John said.

7

I had to agree with him. Granted, bigfoot generally stood head and shoulders above the dogmen in the woods, and they were certainly bigger in stature, but the dogmen were or seemed to be, much more vicious. Sharp teeth, long claws, and a ravenous appetite. But nonetheless, they were somehow controlled by them.

"John, you know what I just thought of?" I asked moving to the edge of my chair.

"What's that partner?" he asked.

These bigfoot had to have been here all along. I was just thinking of the situation as a whole and everything we learned from Ashton. He said that he and his wife ran from the hyena looking dog man and it didn't chase them. Connie was in the car, and it didn't come after her out of the tree line. The only time these dogmen made any kind of threatening maneuvers towards us, is when we were in the woods right, so since that is the case, bigfoot had to have been here. No doubt about it now." I explained excitedly.

"So, the one you shot, that did break that line, absolutely had to have gone rogue. But that still poses a problem for us. It didn't die after being shot in the face. Does that mean that any of them can be killed at all? John asked.

I had thought about that time and time again. I never could come up with a logical explanation for that one. None of this is logical anyway.

"Maybe we won't be able to. Maybe, they must be killed by bigfoot. Look, I know that sounds crazy but honestly John, this is all crazy. I think we have to start looking at this a little more outside of the box than we have been. We come from a logical state of mind, and this is so illogical it isn't even funny. Knowing what we do now, we need to look at this differently. I think that will help us in the long run. Probably not to defeat the dogmen ourselves but trusting that somehow bigfoot can."

John slowly rocked in his rocking chair trying to process everything I had just told him. I knew it was a stretch, but we've done everything else. We are after all, dealing with not one but two creatures that aren't even supposed to exist. Much less, both on the same property.

"We need to get back out into the woods to investigate but I think we should go during the day at first. I know dogmen come out during the day but, not quite as often as they do in the cover of darkness. They'll be more cautious and not so apt to attack us. There is no time to waste." John said.

The next morning as soon as the sun rose over the horizon, we all met up at our house. Marie was set up in the kitchen with a walkie for communication and John, Connie, and I, were geared up and ready to set off into the wood line. We gave a few brief instructions to Marie, and we left. We had looked online for what others had found when it came to bigfoot. Tree structure examples, broken tree limbs, what possible nests look like, we hungered for everything we could get our hands on in relation to these two cryptids.

"Now remember," John said as we drove the short drive to the wood line, "This is a scouting mission only. We aren't going in to kill anything at all unless it comes at us first. Ashton will be here tomorrow night. That's when we'll hopefully be able to hunt to kill. Today, we're simply looking for signs of bigfoot mainly but maybe, we'll stumble on something that shows dogmen in the same areas as well."

We trekked the rough terrain off trail. It was so much thicker this way than on a normal trail that was made, but bigfoot doesn't follow trails...unless they're game trails that is. Most of the encounters my grandpa had were when he went off trail to hunt deer. He would always come back home covered in scratches from briar bushes, covered in mosquito bites, and crawling with ticks. My grandma always gave him down the country for it too, but he never let it stop him. I remember as a child when I would go there on my summer breaks from school, that I always stayed on the trail.

I didn't want any part of what my grandma would dish out if I didn't. I never had one single encounter with them. Maybe that's why. I stayed on the trail; they knew I was there, and they didn't want me to know where they were.

Scouting off trail was the way to go in that case. That would give us the best chance to find some of these tree structures or anything else related to them. We would also have the best chance of maybe sneaking up on one like Connie and I did that day, that is, if that was a bigfoot and not a bear. We made it the long way to the water. John instantly froze when he saw it. I understood because this was the first time he had been back to this place since that dreadful night when we looked hell right in the face.

"Are you okay to keep going John?" I asked seeing the fear emanating off him.

We all stood still until John was good to go forward. He took a few deep breaths and we moved along. The rain had washed all the blood away so there was literally nothing left of that night except our trauma, memories, and our own account of what happened to us. We knew that no one would believe us except those we had already told who had also experienced that. I don't know if I would even be brave enough to go onto one of the encounter shows we had listened to. However, based off others courage to tell their story, we ourselves had learned a lot. Connie had walked ahead of John and I and we saw her leaning over at a nearby tree limb.

"What do you got there, Connie?" I asked walking up to her.

"These tree limb breaks are so inconclusive. How can you really tell what did this" she asked as she lifted the broken portion of the tree limb up.

"Well, it's not the whole tree limb, it's just a portion of the limb that's broken," John said. "But, I agree, it's hard to say with any certainty. Let's keep moving ahead and see if we can find something else."

We had walked quite away through the brush and right in the midst of her walking, Connie froze and pointed. "The cave," she exclaimed. "No, we're too close, we must turn around. We are right at their front door."

John and I walked over and hid behind a big boulder and looked over at the cave. We must've walked clear around the opposite way and are looking at the cave from the other side.

There wasn't any movement at all from the inside. No noises, no smells. The fact that there could've been close to ten dogmen in there, really hit home with us. Just then, we saw one on all fours, make its way to the front of the cave from the side. We all knelt down so it wouldn't see us.

"It must be protecting them so they can sleep. I think I read somewhere that sasquatch had what someone called "day watchers," to protect the ones who sleep. I think that's what this one is doing." John whispered.

That dog man on all fours, had a shoulder height of at least three to four feet tall. Once it stood up, it would be much taller. We had to figure out a way to get out of there before it caught wind of us.

"We need to start working our way back home now," Connie said. "I don't like this at all. I think we may be out of range for the walkie talkie because we haven't heard anything from Marie."

The fear on Connie's face was very clear. At times, when something scared her, she would get angry. I could see it building. I stood in front of her and made her stop for a minute to just breathe.

"I know, seeing one is terrifying. Seeing one in broad daylight is even worse. Just take a second."

"Mark, we may not have a second until this thing smells us. We have to go now." Connie said angrily.

She took off, not being quiet at all. She was snapping twigs and breaking branches as she swiftly moved along. That's all it took. This dog man snapped its head around and scanned the area where we were. It let out a loud howl and then headed in our direction.

"Mark, Connie, Run! It's coming!" John yelled.

No need to be quiet anymore. We took off out of there like a bat out of hell. We ran as hard as we could. We heard it coming through the trees. Snarling echoed behind us, and it felt as if any minute would be our last.

We made it back to the water and quickly stopped to take a break and catch our breath as much as we could since the noises had lessened. John had also reached out to Marie to let her know what happened. Shortly afterwards though, we started feeling small pelts hitting against our back packs. We all looked around confused. Nothing. We then looked up thinking it was just something natural falling from the trees. However, none of the trees we were surrounded by, dropped anything like acorns or pinecones or anything like that. But still yet, the pelts kept coming. Little stones then began hitting the water. It was almost like it was raining rocks every so often. Then the smell hit all of us. The smell that we had smelled the first day in the woods.

"It's here," Connie said as she eyed our surroundings with her weapon drawn. "Now, is it that dog man or is it bigfoot?

I couldn't answer that question for her, and neither could John. The fact of the matter is, is that the day we smelled it, we couldn't figure out what it was then either. We just simply left. That was our plan on this day too. We quickly retreated and made it back home. I was discouraged that we didn't get all our trail cams out, but I was glad that out of twelve of them, we had at least put out nine. We had a possible bigfoot tree break but nothing conclusive with bigfoot. We did find a different way to get to the cave. Then being chased by a dog man...again. Afterwards, at the water, what was throwing small rocks at us and in the water? Was that bigfoot? I don't see dog man standing around throwing things at us after it had been violently chasing us. They would more than likely have just finished the job and attacked us. I couldn't wait for Ashton to come tomorrow night.

I woke up the next morning excited to get the day started. A lot of people would call us crazy. If anyone had heard us talking about this, they would swear we had lost our minds. Before all this started, I would've been the same way. But I have come to grips with this lifestyle, maybe not the cryptid jungle as Connie called it but no matter what is going on out here, I knew that she and I belonged here. I could feel it. The day was longer than normal, and I knew why. It was hot and muggy so when the sun sets this evening, it will be great. John and Marie came over a little after four that afternoon.

We all had an early dinner together and gathered everything we would need before Ashton and his wife showed up. Connie and I had taken down all the trail cams from around our property earlier in the day. We also went out and got more walkie talkies. After everything was collected and loaded up, Connie went in and made coffee for Marie and Ashton's wife.

Not long after, they showed up. They both came to the door, and we welcomed then in. Ashton shook our hands and introduced himself to Marie since she wasn't there when he first came over.

"This is my wife, Sabrina." Ashton said.

We all introduced ourselves and made our way to the kitchen. "I made some fresh coffee," Connie said to Sabrina. "Please, make yourself at home. If you need anything at all, just let Marie know and she'll help you.

Everything was ready to go, and I was chomping at the bit to get into the woods. I threw my pack on my back and went out front to wait for everyone else. About ten minutes later, they all piled out the door and we were off. We climbed in the truck and drove to the wood line. We sat and waited until the sun had almost set. The cool breeze felt nice as we got out of the truck. Truth be told, I had already started sweating just under the weight of my pack and the camo I had put on.

"We came out earlier in the day yesterday. I hadn't thought that we were going to find anything, but I was wrong. We did find a possible tree break from a bigfoot, but we weren't sure if it was from them or just another animal walking by and breaking it. We also found an alternate route to the opposite side of the cave.

That's when everything blew up. Then, we experienced something that was strange. A pungent smell by the water and something was pelting us and the water with small rocks.

"So, how exactly did everything "blow" up though?" Ashton asked.

I explained everything that happened. Ashton looked around and said, "Well, well, that does add a degree of difficulty for tonight. As far as what you said earlier, it could indicate bigfoot with the tree break. I can't be sure, but it's very common that they also throw things at people. No one really knows why though. It could be them saying they recognize you're there or even that you're interrupting a hunt. Did you happen to hear any grunts or calls when you guys were out here, outside of being chased by a snarling dog man. Before that, did you hear anything?"

"Nothing like that Ashton," John said. "It was as quiet as could be. Come to think of it, there weren't any noises at all, nothing from insects or any other type of animal."

He was right. I never even picked up on that. But that's true. We completely missed that. If something large is moving through the woods, everything else will be silent.

"This is where Mark and John encountered that dogman face to face. Connie said as we stood near the water.

John sighed. "If you look through this opening, his whole head filled up that clearing. He was blacker than black, fur covered in blood, red eyes, sharp teeth, and his breath was so hot."

"Then I shot it in the face," I said. "It should have been laying just over that large mound of dirt at the bottom. Should be. But it wasn't."

"Yeah, this whole thing sounds bizarre," Ashton said as he looked around. "It's a little quieter than I would prefer now. It could only mean they're around. Them or the bigfoot. Maybe even both"

"Let's start getting the rest of these trail cams up, please," Connie said. "The first one should go here and around that tree facing toward the clearing."

"Yes, you can't see it because it's so dark, but if you look straight out, you can see the cave, half a mile from here." John said.

We hung up two trail cams in that area because it's the closest to our house and our property. We hung up the last one up near the water. Whether it's dogmen or bigfoot hanging around for the fish, we should get a picture of it. Then hopefully it'll stay in the woods. We prayed it would anyway.

We carefully made it to where we found the tree break earlier and Ashton agreed that we couldn't be positive if that was done on purpose or by another animal in the woods. You know, the kind that belong here. Asheton hung up one of his trail cams at that tree too since it was near the cave on the opposite side.

"Let me ask your opinion." Ashton. "The other night, Connie and I were sitting out on the back deck and one of these dogmen came tearing through the woods in our directions. It broke the barrier, and all our halogen lights came on. But then, we heard a bigfoot yell. I am sure that's what it was. It wasn't a howl; it was a yell. As soon as that happened, the dogman backed off and went back into the woods. It never came after us. After that we ran inside. So, I was putting two and two together, or trying to. The only thing that makes sense, is that somehow these bigfoot creatures are controlling the dogmen. They have to be. They're keeping them in the wood line. The one that came out that you and John had seen while hunting and the one that scratched your house, had to be a rogue. We also thought the one I shot, had to have been the rogue too. Have you ever heard such a thing?"

"I can't say that I ever have," Ashton said curiously. "That of course doesn't mean that's not a thing, I just hadn't heard of it. But there aren't too many things about this topic that adds up."

Connie reached out and hastily grabbed my arm. "Do you hear that," she asked in a panicked tone. "It's something heavy moving out in front of us. It's going to get us, Mark, we have to go now." She yelled.

I reached over and quickly covered her mouth before she had the chance to yell again. "Look, you're not new to this. You have to be quiet. Yes, this is a massive beast but it's also an animal of some sort. Handle this as you would a normal hunting trip. You wouldn't dare yell like that."

I removed my hand from her mouth. She was breathing heavily, and fire flew from her eyes in anger. A loud tree knock broke the tension of the situation.

"What the-?" Ashton said.

"Bigfoot," I said, "Listen, the footfalls are retreating away from us."

Two more knocks followed and then once again, everything fell as silent as it was when we first got there.

Ashton looked at me in surprise. "I told you; they control them. It's like a knock of the trees keeps the danger away from us." I said.

Ashton let out a small whoop into the darkness and he got a grunt in return. We walked maybe a mile further into a clearing behind us and found what appeared to be a footprint. But before we could examine it. A middle-sized tree got pushed over.

"We're too close, we have to back out of here." Ashton said.

There was no time to explain as we stood and listened to a different thrashing sound. Ashton's eyes were huge even in the cover of darkness.

"They're coming, get out now!" he exclaimed.

We all ran with wreck less abandon. We made it out with no time to spare. Larger rocks were flying through the woods at us with narrow misses. It was no longer small pebbles; these were like small boulders. What the heck did we come across? Why did bigfoot turn on us like that? If any of those rocks had hit us, we would've been knocked unconscious. We were too close to what? We stopped once the rocks were no longer being thrown and the woods had once again fallen silent.

"What were we too close to, Ashton, and why in the hell did they start throwing small boulders at us?" I asked as I desperately tried to catch my breath.

Ashton gulped down some water and wiped his mouth and face with the bottom of his t-shirt. "Obviously, there's something special with that place. We could've been close to their home, it could've been a birthing site or, they could've had their young up there in like a nursery. We were far into the woods. We had to have stumbled up on something like that to get that kind of reaction out of them that was negative. Generally, they're docile in nature unless they feel threatened."

Connie had sat down on the ground in a clearing of dirt to rest. I felt bad for bringing her on this expedition. This may have entirely diminished her love for nature, hunting, hiking. I really didn't want that for her. These encounters were a heavy burden to carry. I knew that mentally; it was also taxing.

"Come in," Marie said over the walkie talkie. "Are you guys okay; we haven't heard anything from you."

John cued up his walkie. "Yeah, we're good. Had some pretty close calls but right now, we're alright. How are things there?"

"That's another reason we wanted to contact you," Sabrina said. "There's been some strange noises outside. Screeching, almost like a hawk, but this was no bird I had ever heard before. It was almost like an imitation."

I was hoping the girls would be okay there. I knew that they wouldn't dare come out, especially now with strange noises outside. But neither of them that I knew of, knew how to handle a weapon and even if they did, I didn't think they would ever shoot something. That wasn't their nature.

"We have to start walking back," Ashton said, "Bigfoot will make those imitation calls."

I didn't think that bigfoot would do anything to harm them. Of course, I also hadn't had a bigfoot throw a rock the size of my head at me either. This was all so unpredictable now. The bigfoot of these woods seemed to be safer than the dog man. Less threatening for sure. Minus the rocks that is. We would have to leave the area and let everything settle before we came back during the day to get the trail cameras. As we were walking out, a sound that I never wanted to hear again, echoed across the vast openness of the forest of trees, laughter. What in the hell could be out here laughing?

"That's a damn hyena," John said as we all stood in bewilderment. The sound had carried from the cave to where they were standing.

Connie just hung her head. "I can't take this. We have bigfoot, dogmen and now a hyena?"

Ashton paced back and forth. He reminded us of a professor trying to figure out the answer to a long scientific equation.

"Me and Sabrina saw a dog man that looked like a hyena. John, didn't you say that you saw one that looked like a hyena too?" Aston asked.

"I sure did, through the binoculars the night Mark shot that black one." John answered.

"So, let's reason it from there because how likely is it that you guys have a hyena roaming around as well?" Ashton said.

Connie chuckled. "How likely is it that we have two cryptid creatures roaming here that shouldn't even exist?

No way he would be able to argue his way out of that one. The likelihood that any of the three would be there should be low. But here we were, in the middle of the woods chasing two of the three of them.

"Are you proposing that the dog man that looks like a hyena is making that cackling noise?" I asked.

Connie stood up from where she was sitting and started walking around. She was stressing. I could see it. I needed to get her back home so she could decompress from this whole situation. We all made our way back down the mountain. The cackle rang out again. Connie never missed a beat. She was a strong hunter, but this was too much.

"There's a loud banging sound coming from the back of the house," Marie yelled into the walkie. "Like a baseball bat hitting something metal."

8

John and I looked at each other. "My cattle I yelled, it's in the backyard. I've not ever seen anything metal out here in the woods. That must be what it is.

"Hold your positions," John told Marie sternly, "We're nearly there."

Ashton took off running ahead of us. Connie followed quickly in his footsteps, and John and I weren't too far behind them.

Finally, the exit! We all jumped in the truck and sped off to the house. Connie ran inside to get what had gone on while we were in the woods from Sabrina and Marie while John, myself, and Ashton cautiously went around back. We held our flashlights up as we walked around the side but put them away once we saw that the lights were on lighting up the whole area. We checked on the chickens in the coop. They were all accounted for, then we made our way to the cows. They were fine. We made our way to the pigs which were fine as well, however the large metal container we had for their water, had big dents in it. That had to have been what was making that noise.

But what would come here and do that? Once you step foot in the yard the lights come on. So, they had to have been on when this thing was beating the container. But where were the girls when this started?

"We had come into the living room to watch television. Nothing had happened so we didn't really see a need to just sit in the kitchen, so we closed the curtains and came in here. Plus, watching television would distract us from what could possibly be going on with you guys." Marie said.

"Shortly after we came in here though," Sabrina said, "That's when we heard that strange screeching noise. After we talked to you guys on the walkie talkie, about ten to fifteen minutes had gone by and that's when we heard the banging noise. We just stayed in the living room and called you guys again."

After me and the guys had finished looking everything over outside and making sure everything else was secure with no further damage, we came inside. The girls were all sitting in the living room talking. They went over with us everything they had told Connie and what they experienced. We also filled them in on what happened in the woods.

"It laughed?" Sabrina asked surprised.

Ashton sat down beside her. "Yep, it sure did. You would've thought a person was out there in the woods."

"Now, I've done research on wild animals when I was looking up all this stuff with the dog man. I was trying to understand what their habits may be based off other animals. I had run across those images of the seven dog men and when I found the one that looked like a hyena, I decided to investigate that one further since I had seen it. In comparison with actual hyena, this one is obviously much larger but maintains a lot of the same characteristics. The laugh being some-thing I heard mentioned on one of the encounter stories I had listened to. If you look into the hyena in the wild, they laugh out of frustration or conflict. I'd say we caused it some frustration by being there." John went on to explain everything that he could remember.

I was impressed with John's acquired knowledge of at least this one hyena dog man. We would need all we could get. I can't wait to get those trail cameras back. Hopefully there's something on there we can see and maybe they'll keep these things away from our home.

"Did you guys find anything out back when you looked that could've been making the noise they heard?" Connie asked.

"Yeah, we did actually. All the animals are fine, none of the enclosures are damaged. But the water trough we have for the pigs is dented all to hell. That's where that sound was coming from. The lights were all on when we got back there meaning whatever did this, did this in full light."

"This is all our fault," Marie said, "If we would have stayed in the kitchen or even left the curtains open, we would've seen it."

John walked over and sat beside her. "Please, it's okay, I would prefer you didn't see it that close whether it was a bigfoot or a dog man. The main thing is you guys are alright, the animals are alright and we are too."

The actions still didn't add up. Why would something risk being seen just to bang on a water trough? Maybe it was a dominant behavior, but that would be more indicative of a bigfoot I would think, even a younger one at that. I don't really think a dog man would do something like that. It would all fine in line with the screeching noises as well. Imitations of birds, hawks maybe, possibly the screech of an owl. I know that's a common thing they do. Everything adds up, the more you think it through, to it being a bigfoot that came through while we were gone. I wonder though; was this behavior a result of us getting too close to whatever it was in the woods? We had talked about all the scenarios for hours it seemed before we realized how late it had gotten.

"You guys are welcome to stay the night," Connie said to Ashton and Sabrina, "We have a pull-out sofa bed."

"With all due respect," Sabrina began, "I think we're going to stay the night with John and Marie."

Connie chuckled. "Well, I understand that one, you've lived through enough when this was your home."

They all gathered their things and went back to John and Marie's. Connie and I went to bed shortly after, but I just laid there in bed, unable to sleep, going over everything we'd seen and experienced since we moved there. I was frustrated that this couldn't have been everything she and I had planned while we sat in our apartment in the city. We had so many visions and none of them included sharing our home or our land with these things.

I woke up early the next morning, had a shower, and fixed coffee. I knew that we had just put those cameras up last night, less than twenty-four hours ago, but with everything going one while we were there, I wanted so badly to go see if anything was on them. Surely with all the activity, something had to have been stirred up enough to end up on one of them and we had all the cameras in places we've had activity every time we'd been in the woods.

I called John and asked if it would be foolish to go check. All I would need to do is bring the laptop up there to check the Sd card.

"You are a real glutton for punishment aren't you, Mark?" John asked.

He wasn't wrong. I was fully vested in these creatures, all of them. I admit, almost obsessed. More importantly, I wanted to sit outside at our house anytime day or night without being or feeling threatened. I knew that would never happen until this problem was solved. The longer we waited, the longer it would take and even though I am a very patient person, my patience was beginning to run thin.

"Mark," Connie laughed, "You can't really think that something is on the cameras already. You know they take a little longer than that."

I sighed. "I know, but I'm just factoring in all the activity we had. The bigfoot moving around, that dog man, goodness only knows what else. I just feel we need to look."

Connie sat down beside me and rubbed my shoulder. "Give it a few days, yeah? We'll go check them when they've had more time to capture something. We don't know exactly how these creatures operate or their habits. Let's just keep an eye out here at home and see if any of the activity has diminished with the cameras being in the woods."

I guess deep down I knew she was right, but the thought still tugged at me. Maybe it was all wishful thinking on my part that we could have the cameras up for one night and instantly have proof of these beings. Of all the accounts I had heard, no one who had set cameras out ever caught anything and the ones that did, the photos were blurry, inconclusive, or said to be a hoax. I knew that even natural animals in the woods didn't go straight to the cameras. So, once again, I pushed everything aside and went on about my day and started doing things that needed to be done. The days went by, and I thought that what John had told us about the cameras had turned out to be right. There hadn't been any activity on our property, the lights haven't come on, everything was pretty quiet.

I know that generally, Connie and I waited for a while to check our cameras but after a few weeks, I couldn't take it anymore. She and I went out early one morning, took the laptop, our weapons, and some water and headed to the cameras. Connie was humoring me in going and truth be told, she probably wanted me to go so I would finally be quiet about it. We checked the trail cam that was furthest from our property, nearest to the cave. We were especially careful not to disturb anything and we were as quiet as humanly possible, so we didn't draw attention to us by any dog man or bigfoot. I knelt down, hands shaking with excitement and adrenaline. I just knew that something had to be on this one because this camera was on the tree closest to where we were having small boulders thrown at us and the dog man chasing us. We saw plenty of deer as we clicked through the photos, but that was all. To say I was deflated would be an understatement. But I knew it was a long shot.

We checked all the trail cameras and finally made it to the water. "Last camera," Connie said. "Fingers crossed."

What we saw on that last trail camera was something we hadn't expected to see. Sure, there were deer and racoons, you know, the normal things you see in the woods, but the last two pictures made us both gasp. It was a man. He was sitting in the dirt, legs crossed, right where I shot that dog man. His back was towards the camera in the first picture we saw him and the last picture, he had turned to face the camera. It was almost like he knew it was there even though we had tried to make them as inconspicuous as possible. We had a clear shot of his face though. We saved those two pictures, set everything back up, and went home. We went to John and Marie's to show them the pictures to see if they knew who this man was. No doubt, this was not normal. Why would anyone just go and sit in the woods in the middle of the night?

"There was a man," John asked. "Why would anyone just sit in the pitch black, in the woods alone? I wonder if they know about what's going on and if they do, why would they put themselves at risk like that?"

I pulled up the pictures for Marie and John.

"John, I just thought about something," Connie said. "Is there another way into these woods from somewhere else or is it just the entrance that's a couple miles from our house?"

She was right. I hadn't heard any vehicle pass by our house. Of course, if this was in the middle of the night, I don't guess we would have. But it was still a good question. I never thought about there being another way into the woods.

"As far as I know," he replied, "It's just by yall's place. But I also haven't really had a reason to look. When Marie and I came here, we were happy just to be here. I never ran across anything else while hunting as far as roads out of here or anything else. I never really had to go too far in to get what I needed."

Connie and I both looked at each other. I knew what she was thinking. One or both of us would have to stay up to see if anyone passed by to go to the woods. The time stamp on the photo was just before three in the morning. The witching hour. Great.

"Maybe what we should do is talk to Ashton and see if he had ever seen him. If this man is frequenting these woods and assuming the only entry is by passing our property, maybe they know who it is or have seen him walk by." I suggested.

John walked to the other room to grab his cell phone to call them.

"What if he's just a homeless man?" Marie asked.

That could be a possibility and I have to admit that I didn't think about that as an option. But if that's the case, someone still needs to let him know in a tactful manor, that the woods aren't safe because by simply sitting out there, he's putting himself in very grave danger. John walked back into the room before we could finish that conversation.

"I'm sending Ashton a picture of these photos. He said he didn't recall seeing anyone walk past their house, however that doesn't mean he didn't. He said he wouldn't know for sure unless he could see what he looked like."

It would possibly work by sending him the photos but it's a picture of a picture, they don't always turn out too well. But nonetheless, it was sent and now all we could do was just wait.

A phone call was not retuned, however. Ashton showed up at the door to John and Marie's about thirty minutes later. We were all surprised to see him and was wondering why he didn't just call.

"That's the guy we bought the house from that used to live there," he said as he sat down and took his phone out. "I would recognize him anywhere. He's peculiar, a little weird, definitely has his quirks. But he is a nice man overall. His name is Henry Webb. He's probably in his sixties I would say. I don't know why he would have been out in the woods just sitting there. That doesn't make any sense."

"Yes, he's the one you were telling us about the day after this creature stole a chicken, right," I said. "You said he had told you that having animals on that property wasn't a good idea."

Ashton shifted in his seat. "That's correct. I bet we have figured out now, why that is. There's dog man and Bigfoot on that property and he knew it."

We all looked at one another and I knew that we all had the same question running through our minds. Why would he be sitting out there in the middle of the woods at night, knowing there are these cryptid entities that could easily kill him? I knew Ashton said he was peculiar and had his quirks and flaws, but that's a little much if you ask me.

"Do you have any way of getting in touch with him, Ashton?" John asked.

"I don't have his number, no," Ashton said disappointedly. "I have no way of getting in touch with him at all, actually. Once he left the property, that was the last I saw of him until you sent me this picture. He seemed relieved to be leaving."

Connie had stood up and began pacing. "What has me baffled is I'm sure what has everyone baffled after hearing that. Why, why did he come back if he was glad to be rid of the property and secondly, why is he now putting himself in harm's way just sitting there like that? By the looks of it, he didn't have a care in the world out there. He certainly didn't seem to be afraid. We have to figure out some way to get his information so we can talk to him to see if we can answer any of these questions."

Connie was right. We wouldn't be able to put any of the pieces to this puzzle together without Mr. Henry Webb. The days passed by, however and we couldn't find anything out on him. These days, people locked up their contact information good and tight. Landlines were almost nonexistent, and he may not even have a cell phone. Some people do and some don't. That only left two things for us to try and do.

We were going to have to keep an eye on the trail cameras to pick up a pattern and we would also have to camp out to try to talk to him. The good thing is, he would have to pass our house to get there so there wouldn't be a need to stay in the woods. We were gearing up to go check the trail cameras early one morning. It had been eerily quiet with no activity on the property.

No sounds from the woods, no harassment of our animals, no wild calls. I was hopeful that these cameras were doing what we had set them out for and that it wasn't just a fluke. Connie and I were even able to sit out on the back deck one night and stargaze. She and I opened the door to leave and there on the porch, sat Henry Webb. We were both taken aback. He stood up to greet us and stuck out his hand.

"The name's Henry Webb, it's nice to meet you fine folk. How are you likin' this here house?" he said in a strong southern drawl.

Henry was stout, maybe five foot ten. He had a longer beard, but it seemed neatly kempt, but it was all grey. He had dark rimmed glasses and a sideways smile that stretched across his aging face. He looked a lot less scary than he did on the trail camera. I was glad for that. Connie and I glanced at each other in disbelief. How was he here? We had looked for him all over the place. Did we somehow put some kind of shockwave out into the universe to manifest him here? That was silly I knew but I didn't know how else to explain it. I shook his hand, oddly staring at him all the while.

"Well, you look like you done seen a ghost, boy. Are you okay?" he said as he chuckled.

Connie walked over to break the tension. "Yes, were okay, you just caught us by surprise that's all. Look, I don't mean to be forward or strange when I say this, but we have been looking all over for you."

Henry scratched his balding head. "You've been looking for me, why's that?" he asked.

I was confused. Clearly, he saw the trail camera that took his picture. He looked right at it. He would've had to have known that we would've pulled the pictures and questioned why he was on our property in the middle of the night.

"Well, Mr. Webb," I began, but he interrupted me.

"Mr. Webb was my father, please, call me Henry." He said.

I started again. "Henry, we know you have been on our property. We pulled the pictures, and you were sitting in a very dangerous place. We were concerned for your safety and also curious as to why you were there that late at night. We enlisted the help of our friends in showing them the picture of you so maybe we could figure out who you were and why you were there. The man you sold the house to had talked about you in the past with us. He is the one who identified you."

Henry smiled, "Yes, he was a real nice fella. He had a good-looking family too. But I warned him about the animals. It's not a good idea, ya know. I saw you had way more back there than he did when I came by the other night, so I stopped to give you guys a warning as well."

"I'm intrigued, Henry, do tell. One, why shouldn't we and two, why do you think it's okay to go onto our property and just sit there." I said, interested to see what he had to say.

Henry sat back down, and Connie and I joined him.

9

His breath was ragged as he began. "I know you know already, but I'll humor you anyway. I first moved here when I was nearing twenty-five years of age. My beautiful bride and I shared a lot of memories in this house right here. We raised two strapping young men, and I taught them everything I knew about hunting and fishing. It was then that we first realized we weren't alone.

On one particular hunting trip, the boys and I were trailing a deer. One of the biggest bucks we'd ever seen. I was so proud when my oldest boy had shot it. I don't know, I guess this thing smelled it as the deer ran leaving the scent of blood everywhere. We had heard a snarling growl in the distance. We looked for this deer everywhere hoping it had fallen somewhere close. The thing is, the growls got closer and louder."

I could see him starting to tremble as he recalled this vivid memory from years ago almost like it had just happened. He was traumatized for sure. I told him he didn't have to go on, but he persisted.

"We pushed ahead, not willing to let this deer go. It would've given us meat for a good bit. We trudged ahead as the cold wind started to blow harder through the trees. A whistle came from somewhere in the woods echoing almost through the whole valley. We paused in our tracks. The trees began to sway, and the growl was moving further away but what we saw step out from behind a large oak tree, we didn't ever expect. Bigfoot. As plain as day and I swear on my life. I know how crazy it sounds but it was there, and we saw it. The boys screamed, I just stood there in shock. The bigfoot ran back into the woods and disappeared. We saw the deer just then, close to where this bigfoot was. We hesitantly made our way to the deer, shaking the whole time. I didn't know if it was going to reach out and grab us or not, but we hadn't heard anymore movement. We drug the deer out of there. I couldn't get my boys back in the woods after that."

Connie and I sighed and told him about our experiences with bigfoot. Then, we asked him about the dog men. He acknowledged them as well.

"So why in the world would you sit alone in the woods at night knowing they're there, then," Connie asked. "Aren't you afraid they'll attack you because surely, what we experienced out there is real and they are predators."

Silence filled the air as he searched for the right words. He was only able to stammer out his reply. "I have nothing left. The woods right there are where my best memories are. I come out at night because no one will be there. I just sit there and reminisce on the good time with my boys. I know I wanted to move as soon as they grew up and had their own lives. I didn't want my wife around that. That's when I sold the house. But I told that boy not to have animals. It would bring in the monsters, and he had too nice of a family to have them experience that too. I didn't tell him monsters lived here though. One, he wouldn't have believed me and two, he wouldn't have bought the house. I can only assume he didn't listen since he moved as well."

I motioned for Connie to call John and John called Ashton. They arrived at our house shortly after. Ashton and John sat and talked to Henry and Ashton told Henry of what he had experienced before they moved. Connie came out and bought glasses of iced tea for us.

"We need to figure out how to get rid of these awful creatures,

Henry. Would you be willing to help us, clearly you don't fear them." Connie said.

Henry chuckled. "I know you think you can get rid of them, but you can't. The bigfoot of the woods, they're your only hope. That's what saved me and the boys that day. The bigfoot whistle.

That's how I think I keep them away when I go sit in the woods. I whistle. I hear movement but no growling. I like to think I call the bigfoot in for protection. It's like my special power."

There's the crazy quirks Ashton was talking about. I was waiting for them to appear. I'm not doubting any of Henry's story. But having "Bigfoot powers" takes it a little far.

"Would you be willing to go out with us as a group," John asked. "We have all the necessary equipment. Stuff I'm know you never used forty years ago."

As we sat waiting for his reply, a howl came from deep within the trees that shook all of us to the core.

"Well," Henry said. "I think whatever that was, just made my mind up for me. Let's chase this son of a bitch outta here."

We had given John and Ashton time to get geared up and ready and into the woods we went. We quickly made it to the water and Henry went on to tell us where he sat and reminisced the memories he and his boys had shared there. We couldn't stay long of course, whatever it was that howled didn't sound too far away from our house.

"Have you guys ever thought about setting up camp out here and staying overnight," Henry asked. "My boys and I did that often. We would lay out under the stars, roast marshmallows, and just talk. I think I miss those moments most of all."

I don't know if I would feel comfortable setting up camp and staying out here all night long. Especially after our run in with bigfoot and the rock escapade recently. Not to mention, large snarling, oversized dog men. From the looks on everyone else's face, they shared my opinion.

"You're a braver man than I am," John said. "No way you would catch me out here in the overnight hours."

Henry laughed at that. I had a suspicion that he had experienced many things in his life. Most of which wouldn't go over well with us. In his time, I'm sure, things were significantly different.. I would also think that he didn't experience what he had with his sons. We took Henry around everywhere that we had been. He showed us exactly where he and his sons were at when they had their encounter. I don't know what I would've done had I been in his position. I probably would've left the deer and high tailed it out of there. But I wasn't in his shoes so I couldn't really speak on that.

"I wouldn't be opposed to doing something like that, however, I don't think my wife would be keen on the idea. What we experienced the other night was terrifying, that I'll admit, but it would give us more insight on their habits at night." Ashton spoke up.

Connie looked at him like he had five heads. "You have got to be kidding me. You would stay out here?"

I couldn't disagree with what he had said. But from what I'd heard on the encounters I had listened to; most researchers came up with nothing if they went out with the intent to find something. Generally, the encounters happened to unsuspecting individuals who had only planned on camping and stargazing. Some just by driving down the road. Not by someone setting up a basecamp and really trying to get to the heart of what's going on.

"Even if I wanted to, not that I do mind you, but you guys know good and well Marie wouldn't let me stay out here either. I would almost have to be like a teenager and sneak out after she went to sleep." John snickered.

Connie shot a sharp glance at me just then. "Don't even think about." She said sternly.

Just then, another howl rang through the trees. We were all frozen where we stood. Henry let out a loud, melodic whistle. The noises around us all fell silent. We all stood waiting for something to explode from the trees, but of course nothing did. Henry smiled at us and winked. I knew that didn't mean anything in reality. But if that's what he wanted to believe, that's fine. I'm not going to be the one to burst his bubble. We walked along looking at everything. Henry took us on a different route however, we hadn't ever been this way and I was kicking myself for not knowing that this land is also part of mine and Connie's property. This was unlike any portion that we had been through. I looked at John and he just returned a shrug of his shoulders indicating that he didn't know either. I was more determined than ever now, just by looking at the expansive woods in front of us, that maybe the land closest to the house, was only on the outskirts of where both of these cryptids actually live.

"So, if you go along here," Henry said as he pointed straight ahead. "There's another creek bed. It's a lot shallower than the first one by yalls place but it's nice just the same. Probably about a month after we saw this thing, I came walking back here and found me a footprint. I didn't have anyone to share it with back then, only my boys would believe me. Everyone else would say that I was living up my quirky nature and dismiss it before I even finished the sentence. But this was a weird one. This was shaped like that of a dog. I even said wolf back then mainly because of the sheer size of it."

"I also found a huge wolf print, Henry." Ashton said. "But this wasn't a regular sized wolf though."

Henry cackled and slapped his knee. "You're right about that boy, this isn't a wolf at all. This was from one of those hellhounds. I just didn't know it at the time. I had only seen that one bigfoot."

I started thinking how we would almost have to buy a dozen cameras if not more, to put all the way out here. There were so many ways they can travel through here and we don't even know how many there are of either one of them. If I remember what John told me correctly, bigfoot has family units and based of dogs and wolves themselves, these dog men should be the same if they too like to be in packs. We all stopped and took a break once we reached the creek Henry was telling us about.

"How far back exactly does our property go, Henry? I never knew it came back this far. If this is truly ours, we got more for our money than I thought." I said as I sat down on a large rock by the water.

Ashton walked over and sat down. "I have a confession to make now. I knew about all this back here. This is pretty much where your land stops, just a little further past the creek but that's it. I just wanted to get our family away from here, so I only set the price for what we paid for the house just to get out from under it."

Henry laughed. "That's why you got such a good price, boy. I did the same thing. Except, you got an even better deal than ole Mark did."

"Yeah, we borrowed more than the price of the house because we wanted to do restorations and stuff," Ashton went on. "I didn't know at the time that I was buying a zoo from hell and none of the restorations would be done before having to move."

We sat listening at all the sounds around us and the water run across the rocks. This area really wouldn't be too bad for camping. It was cleared with enough room for a tent and then space leftover for a campfire. It would be peaceful to just hang out here. It left me more determined than ever now, to make our whole property safe and usable. Suddenly, all the noises stopped. The only thing that could be heard, were the breaths that we each took and the water in the creek. Laser focused, we all looked around to see or hear any type of movement. Low chuffs were coming from somewhere in the woods indicating that something knew we were there. All standing now, John, myself, and Connie, drew our weapons.

"That could be coming from either one of these creatures," Henry whispered. "Be ready."

Cautiously, we turned and started walking back, but we weren't alone. Something was pacing us just inside the woods. We all heard it. Henry broke the silence with another whistle. I cut my eyes at him. My adrenaline was pumping through my veins and my patience was wearing thin. I couldn't handle a halfcocked idea that a simple whistle would bring us protection and we could all skip merrily out of the forest. Henry lowered his head sensing my irritation. I almost felt bad but before I had a chance to, the growls came, one from beside us and one directly behind us. We quickly picked up the pace being sure not to run. That would be the worst thing. I didn't realize just how far in we had come. Getting back out was taking longer than it should have. My worst fear crept in. We're lost.

"I don't think this is the right way guys," I said. "It didn't take us this long to get to the creek."

We all stopped and looked around. Henry walked a little way ahead of us. "We walked the same way we came in. We should be fine to go on ahead. It's a straight shot out of here."

I was hot and tired. I was mainly tired of dealing with all the bullshit going on and just wanted things to be normal. I was losing my cool and I felt it, but this was different. Yes, I was all of the aforementioned things however, the anger I felt building inside of me wasn't normal. I've never been this way.

"Hey guys wait up," I said. "I know we don't have time to talk but this is important. Do any of you feel angry or confused, maybe a little disoriented?"

They all looked at me strangely. Maybe this was all me and it was just the heat getting to me.

"Connie, remember when we first came to the water, and I felt something strange when I pulled my gun? I asked you about it when we got back to the house."

Connie thought for a minute. "Yes, I do, you said you felt that if you shot your gun, you would regret it."

"Okay, same way but this time, I'm so angry I could bend steel with my bare hands, and I don't know why."

John walked over to me and put his hand on my shoulder. "You could be picking up the energy from these dog men. Maybe your sensitive to them. It would prove to be useful though. We could tell when they're around that way."

I felt as silly as Henry with his supposed whistling. What a dynamic duo we would be in the woods. This is all preposterous. "So, you guys really don't feel anything at all?"

They all shook their heads no. I was afraid of that. The only thing to do now is keep going in hopes they would leave us alone. We hadn't heard them growl anymore. So, I could only assume we were moving out of what they claim to be as their territory. Henry turned out to be right after all. Not too much longer and we had reached the first creek and the clearing where I shot that wretched beast. That of which, still needed an answer. Do these things really come from another dimension, do they hold certain powers to be able to restore themselves, or do they bury their dead and the one I shot, was put to rest somewhere away from here? None of the answers would be a surprise to me at this point.

"We have to do something," Connie said. "We can come out here hundreds of times, but the result is always the same. We get freaked out by what we already know is here and then we leave. The definition of insanity is doing the same thing over and over expecting a different result. Nothing will be accomplished at this rate. Henry, you said let's chase them out of here and that's what I intend on doing. I know that you say that we ourselves can't get rid of them but, I'm tired of spinning my wheels here."

Henry walked over to where Connie stood. "I agree little lady. Spinning our wheels won't help you or your friends and family. I told you that only bigfoot can get rid of them, and I think that's partly true, but I don't think that's the only way. In fact, I know that's not the only way."

We all looked at Henry confused. Does he know secrets that he hasn't told us yet? Clearly, he knew more than he was letting on and it was high time we get to the bottom of this. Winter would be coming soon, and this is not something we can afford to be dealing with then. Connie and I would have to be able to hunt for meat to sustain us for the colder months. We already had some with the animals we have but I would sure love some deer meat to go along with it.

"So, cut to the chase Henry. I know we just met you, but you know more than what you're telling us. We need to know what's really going on here...all of it." I said to him sternly.

I felt myself getting angrier than ever again. Out of nowhere, my blood started boiling. Then a growl came from the distance. Why is this happening to me every time the dogmen come close to us again? It hadn't happened at all until Henry was around. I didn't feel this when I shot that one, or in the cornfield. All I felt was fear then. But now, everyone could see it. Henry looked at me and then to the ground. He knew. He knew exactly what was happening and it was time to find out the truth of why.

After we made it back to our house, we all sat at the kitchen table eyeing Henry. I had calmed down once again and was ready to learn what was going on here.

"After my boys and I had a run in with that bigfoot, I set out to learn everything I could about them. I went to the library and checked out every book I could get my hands on. I read countless books it seemed. I wasn't ever really into the whole internet thing. Books were always my go to. Anyway, I met a man who noticed my pattern at the library whom eventually, came up to me and asked about it. He said that he had witnessed one himself and went on to tell me about his encounter. That was when I learned about the dog man as well. He said that if you have a bigfoot on your property then no doubt, you also have a dog man. They go hand in hand." Henry said.

John shifted in his chair. "Yeah, I read the same thing when I was doing the research I did as well as listening to those encounter shows. It's like they live together or something."

"Exactly," Henry went on. "He told me that there was a way to keep them all away but that it would be a little risky. At that point, I was willing to do anything. I wanted to protect my wife and I also wanted to have that time back with my boys in the woods. Armed with that knowledge, I went to the woods and did what that man said. It would be something I would grow to regret however."

10

I could only begin to assume what Henry did was probably an act of evil unbeknownst to him at the time. This was turning into a real-life nightmare.

"A blood sacrifice was necessary. I did what I had to do. A fire, blood, a couple incantations. I wanted my family to be safe. But that man lied to me. I found the print I told you all about shortly after I did all those things. It turned out, that the man I met didn't live too far from me when I lived here. He was obviously having more problems than what we were. The awful deed had been done though. I was stuck. The ritual was actually to call them in. He knew that if he could convince me to do that, it would take them off his property and put them here in these woods."

Connie gasped. "Isn't there some way that you can take it back though, like a reversal ceremony or something? I'm not saying I want that on our property because that's nothing but evil but, is that a possibility to do so that these things go away?"

Before he had a chance to answer Connie, I interjected with my own question. A question I desperately needed an answer to.

"Why do I get so angry when they're around, Henry? It didn't happen in the past when John and I had our run ins or even when I shot that one in the face, which I would also like to ask you about. But the little time that you've been around me in the woods, I get so angry when they're around."

"That is part of it boy, don't you see," he said visibly agitated. "As part of that whole incantation, I threw that bit in there. Whoever was around me at the time in the woods, would have plenty of warning if they ever came. I knew I wouldn't be around anyone, but my boys and I wanted them to be protected just in case. I was trying to plan ahead. Once that was done though, as I said, it brought them here instead of protecting us from them. That dirty bastard made it to where it was then impossible to stay. It became more dangerous over time. It changed our whole way of life. The boys went on to college and moved and I knew me, and my wife would have to leave. I sold this place dirt cheap. I had thought at the time, that whatever was here would stay in the woods because I wouldn't be here to bring them out."

"That's why they can't break the wood line," John exclaimed loudly. "Henry, you're the key to this whole thing!"

It was all starting to make sense. Well, as much sense as it could make. They couldn't leave the wood line because Henry wasn't there. The one that did, that I shot, was obviously something more sinister that a spell couldn't contain. But that still left the question with the bigfoot. Are the bigfoot still controlling the beasts somehow, because the night that Connie and I were on the deck and that dog man reached our property, the bigfoot yelled, and it retreated back into the woods.

"But why me and no one else in the group," I asked. "I would think that whoever was around you, would feel the anger that these dog men put off."

Henry stood up and started pacing. "Honest to goodness bud, I don't have the slightest idea. I can only assume it's because you're the man of the house. You, in a sense, own the property and that means you own everything, not just the land. When yall moved here you took over the role that my boys were supposed to have. I had made that incantation full proof for my sons. At the time, I was planning for their future here. We hadn't planned on moving and once my wife and I passed on, this would be theirs. You took that place. Which means you don't feel any of the anger unless I'm around. They are my heirs, so it would've passed naturally to them. With you, I have to be here."

Ashton had been quite during all of this. I felt bad for him but I'm glad that it was me dealing with this and not him. He was young. I had probably a good twenty years on him. There's no way that he and his family would've been able to handle all of this. It's a lot for me to deal with as well, but I think I would have a firmer grip on it than he would. His goal would be to protect his family. My goal is Connie and myself. That's enough. I don't know how I would even react with a wife plus two younger children. He made the right choice by selling.

"So how do we break this, Henry, how do we make this all go away?" Connie asked.

Henry sat back down and put his head in his hands. "There's only one way and it's not something I thought I would have to do. It's something I didn't want to have to do. Because of this dishonest man, the only way to break the sacrifice I made, is with a sacrifice in return."

"What does that mean, a sacrifice in return? A sacrifice of what?" John asked concerned.

"The sacrifice to break this...is me," Henry said with tears in his eyes. "To put everything back to the way it was and the way it needs to be, is to sacrifice myself. Look, I never thought that it would come down to this. It wasn't supposed to. I made that blood oath on false pretenses. The way this was supposed to go is I would pass this on my sons, the protection, not the curse. I didn't know it was all based on a lie until it was too late. I'm glad we all moved away from this place. Now they don't have to carry this. They're not ever coming back here so this won't ever affect them."

"It's effecting me though, Henry," I yelled. "Now I have to carry this. We have to deal with this on what is now, our land. You can leave anytime you want. But we still have to deal these dog men and bigfoot whether you're here or not. What is the deal with the bigfoot even, why are they here?"

"Well, as you already know, they were here first. They were here I'm sure before we even bought the house. When we encountered what I now know was a dog man, that bigfoot whistled and called them off. I believe that maybe the dog men were trickling in here, but they were able to hold them at bay. That is until I did what I did."

Ashton spoke then. He had been taking all of this information in and processing it the best way he knew how.

"There has to be another way though, Henry. If you made a sacrifice on false pretenses, couldn't you undo it another way other than the traditional sense?" Ashton asked.

Henry was silent. We all were. How was this even reality? I had taken a lot. Bigfoot throwing boulders at our heads, dog men trying to eat us, not being able to enjoy our property. The list is long here. Now, you throw a kooky old man into the mix who supposedly did an incantation in the woods. It all sounds too fantastical to be real. But the fact of the matter is, that it's happening. This isn't a dream, and we are all part of it now.

"Let's do some research on this before we do anything crass," John said. "We have more options than just books at our disposal now. There are also a lot more people who are experiencing this than just us and it wasn't brought on by some ritual done in the woods. I promise you, Henry, you may have brought them here, but you didn't infest the whole world with them. There has to be something out there we can find on this. Maybe, even on the ritual you did and how to reverse it."

Henry looked up at all of us and smiled his crooked smile. I knew he came from a good place. I also knew he was in a rough spot and carrying more than I think I could even handle. Imagine having the weight of protecting your family, strangers, and everything out here on your shoulders. I think I too, would be a little off my rocker at that point. But now that we knew the full story of what was happening. Now came the hard part of having everything go back to the way it was. However, that is.

Connie and I had offered for Henry to stay the night. He went on to tell us that his wife had passed away some years before and he hadn't talked to his sons in a while. They graduated college and have their own lives now and don't want any part of what they left behind, that also included Henry. It made me wonder if maybe he had told them what he had done. Even though it was for their own protection, maybe they just completely wanted to be separated from that. I can't say that I blame them. I did hate it for Henry though.

To go through all of what he did and turn out utterly alone in the end is the worst part of all this for him, I'm sure. I couldn't say that even if we figured out how to break this whatever he did and send the dog men away, that it would repair whatever may have been broken between he and his sons, but at least it would lessen the weight he had been carrying for all these years.

Later that night, Connie and I lay in bed talking about everything. At one point, we even broke out into laughter, not believing what we had been going through and everything we heard could be true. We knew it was though and in our living room, lay a broken, lonely man who had no one but us.

John called me the next morning. He had done research on our property and was eager to tell us.

"Okay, so get this," John began excitedly. "The property attached to yours used to be owned by an Otis P. Welding. That has to be the man that conned Henry. According to the documents, he would be in his seventies now."

I was excited about that, that may mean that he is still alive! Maybe he can help us with Henry and what happened all those years ago.

"Does it say where he's at, John, is he still alive?"

I could hear him pecking on his keyboard. "Yeah, says he's at some retirement home. The land went up for auction once his kids moved him to where he's at now, but no one was interested. So, the county took it over. It doesn't list much about his land, but we more than likely know why no one wanted it. It was probably wrapped in so much lore and evil that no one with even half a brain would take that on. That's also probably why his kids auctioned it."

"Are you up for a road trip, John," I asked with a smile on my face. "He is going to be our best option. We can bring Henry too."

It took right much convincing for Henry to finally agree to go with John and I to see Otis. I knew he was still carrying anger and malice for him, but I assured Henry that John and I would be there the whole time and that Otis may hold the answer to how to get out of this without him having to sacrifice himself in the process.

We loaded up and were off to the Shady Lakes retirement home. It was about an hour's drive from our place, so we had plenty of time to talk on the way. Henry told us that he didn't know too much about Otis. They weren't really friends per se', acquaintances would be the best word for it.

I can't say that I would want to be friends with someone who completely screwed me over either. Just pleasantries exchanged when out in public.

"I saw Otis's kids shortly before my wife and I moved. They were always nice to me. I often wondered if they knew what happened. Since they grew up there, they had to have known about the dog men as well. He probably told them that he got rid of them. I guess in a sense he did, but he did by lying to me and making them my burden to carry instead."

I started wondering if him coming with us was a good idea after all. What if he sees Otis and charges him? That would be a headache and a half that would get us nowhere in this vicious cycle that we were in.

"Now Henry, when we get there, I need you to behave yourself. I know this man did a lot of wrongdoing in your life. But to help you, we need to see if he can tell us how to reverse what you did minus the blood sacrifice of your own life."

He was quiet but I knew that he understood. I looked out the window and wondered how Henry's life would've been had he not done what he did? He and his wife, living out their last moments together on earth knowing their sons were taken care of. Peaceful and happy. I could understand why there was so much angst. Now, Henry was alone, and it didn't have to be that way. We pulled up to Shady Lakes retirement home about twenty minutes later. I once again reiterated to him that he needed to tuck all those feelings away at least for the time being. If he wanted revenge, then get the revenge by reversing the curse. He nodded in agreement, and we went in.

"Yes, we're here to see Otis P. Welding." I said to the lady at the front desk.

She met eyes with me. "Not many visitors for him these days, I'm glad he finally has the company. He's in room one eleven. That's just down the hallway here and to the right."

I thanked her and we started walking. I didn't know which was worse. Being in Henry's position or shoved in this box to live out your final days forgotten about. In a sense, they're both living the same ending. They were both alone. The only difference is that Otis isn't covered with a blood curse so that made Henry's case a little worse. We walked down the sterile hallway. They had different events taped to the walls for the residents to participate in to bring at least some joy to their lives but, it was still an empty feeling all the same.

We turned the corner and found Otis's room just where the lady had said. When we walked in, there we found who we could only presume to be Otis, sitting in a wheelchair facing the window with his backs to us.

I cleared my throat to gain his attention without startling him. "Mr. Welding?"

Otis slowly turned from the window to face us. He met eyes with Henry's, and a scowl covered his face.

"You filthy bastard, you ruined my life." Henry said.

Otis scoffed at what Henry said. "I don't know how you think I ruined your life, Henry. You chose to listen to me so that puts it all on you."

Henry went to rush him, but I quickly grabbed his arm and reminded him that he has to calm down to get the answers we need. Pile driving him out of his wheelchair and into the floor wouldn't help our cause any at all. Henry backed up and stood by us again.

"You knew good and well what that incantation was, and it was all for your own personal gain and none of mine. I have carried this burden for years. My wife has passed away and my boys want nothing to do with me now." Henry said pointing his finger at him.

This conversation would go back and forth forever, neither accepting blame for anything. Arguing and bickering are not getting any questions answered or asked. John looked over at me and rolled his eyes and shrugged.

"Look, Mr. Welding, we came here to actually ask you for your help. Henry doesn't even live on that property anymore; my wife and I do. You know what we have been dealing with and we need to know how to take care of it. Henry has explained everything to me, and I know what went on back then."

Otis rolled himself over to his dresser and pulled out a manilla envelope and laid it on his bed. He motioned for me to come over. He poured out all the contents and went through them. Page after page of what appeared to be information on dog men and bigfoot. He shook the envelope one more time and a necklace fell out. It was tarnished but the amulet on the end was still a shiny purple stone in the middle of a heavy metal ring. I picked it up and held it to the window and the light shimmered through it.

"What's this, Mr. Welding?" I asked.

He held his hand out for me to hand it to him. I laid it in his wrinkled palm, and he laid his other hand over top of it.

"This is what I wore for protection against the dog man that lived on my property. It's the only thing that kept me alive. Whenever they came close, the amulet would glow. I knew by that; it was time to go in. It never failed me." Otis said. "But there's no need me for me to keep any of this anymore. There certainly isn't any dog man that's going to get me in here. Unless you're talking about Nurse Judy who comes to give me my sponge bath." He laughed.

Even Henry couldn't help but crack a smile at that one.

"Now look here, ya old coot," Otis said to Henry, "You can think what you will about me, I'm too old to care now. More than likely, I am going to live out the rest of my days in this facility being taken care of. You still have to fend for yourself. I know that you no longer live there at that house so there's no reason to carry that ole' curse around. You may find what you need in that stack of papers. It had everything in it. All my research from the time I started until I got put in here is there, I don't even remember what it all is. I haven't had a need to look through it and honestly, I haven't cared to. That was from a time long forgotten so, whatever is in there you can use. If the way to break the curse is in there, feel free to send those hellhounds back to my old property. Tell the county to shove it in the process."

We thanked Otis for his time, and we all left, also thanking the lady at the desk as we made our way out. Henry was quiet on the drive back. I could only assume he was taking everything in. I'm also sure that seeing Otis again after so many years was unnerving for him. In his eyes, his life was completely destroyed after meeting him. To be honest, whether Otis wanted to admit it or not, he was responsible. We got back home around dusk and went inside. Connie had prepared us dinner and we all sat eating and talking about the trip to see Otis.

"I know that I led you all to believe I was just as taken aback by these things as ya'll were and I'm sorry for being dishonest. I appreciate you all taking the time to help an ole' kook like me. I didn't want to involve you in any of this and I am sorry that you still are." Henry said.

Connie reached over and laid her hand on his. "We will find a way to break this one way or another. I won't let you sacrifice yourselves for us or anyone else. There has to be another way."

After dinner was cleaned up, we laid the contents of the manilla envelope on the dining room table. We separated the papers into categories. One stack was bigfoot and the other was dog man. I also laid the necklace vertically just across the tops of the two stacks.

"That's an interesting looking necklace," Connie said. "Did this belong to Mr. Welding's wife?"

I tapped the stone and said, "No, he said he actually wore this for protection. Otis said when he wore it and he happened to be around any dog men, that the stone would glow. He said by that, he knew it was time to go back inside. Otis said it never failed him."

"I would be interested to know if it still works," Connie said, "Maybe we could test it out."

I glanced in her direction. I wasn't interested in going on what could be a disastrous trip to see if a stone would save our lives. That's about as preposterous as Henry's whistle thinking it would save him.

"Let's start by looking through all this research that Otis has painstakingly documented first, Connie."

We shuffled through all the papers and Otis's chicken scratch handwriting until we were cross eyed. Henry had given up on finding anything to break the curse about an hour beforehand. I was about ready to be finished myself. None of this was getting us any closer in helping Henry than when we first started. I put all of the papers back in the manilla envelope and slid the necklace in last. I tossed it to the side of the table and went to get a shower. Connie had already left the table and went to the bedroom.

Before bed, I went and checked on Henry. He was sitting up watching television, but he wasn't really paying attention to what was on the screen.

"What's up, Henry, how are you holding up?" I asked as I sat down beside him.

He was quiet for a while, and I just sat with him. I knew this was all taking its toll on him. He's carried this secret around for many years. If anything, the good thing is, he is finally free from at least that burden. He can finally get that off his chest and relax. He's in a safe place here, a place of friends.

"What if we don't find it, Mark," Henry asked, still staring at the television. "What if the only answer is the one, we are trying to avoid?"

I got up and walked to the fridge and grabbed two beers. I handed one to Henry and sat back down.

"We're going to figure this out buddy, don't worry. We'll keep searching until we find the answer."

11

I could only hope that I was right. This wasn't exactly my area of
expertise, and we were all still learning about both of these cryptids. Having Henry show up and finding out he had some blood curse
on him was something we would all also have to learn about, and
quickly. But I could see that, even though we've only just now begun
the search for the answer, that Henry was feeling he should just give
up. He felt like all was lost and there wasn't any hope. I looked over at
him and he had leaned back on the couch and his eyes were closed. I
took the near empty bottle of beer from his hand and covered him
with the blanket and went to bed.

John and Marie came over the next morning and we all sat out on
the front deck drinking coffee and enjoying the sunshine. Henry
walked out a little bit later and joined us. Marie hadn't been with us
for a little bit, so she had to be filled in on everything. John had told
her some things but not all.

"That's so bizarre," Marie said. "What are you guys going to do?"

"The only thing we can do, Marie, just keep hunting so to speak."
John said.

The pigs in the back started squealing which set off the chickens
which in turn set off the cows. We all jumped up. Something had to

be back there. "You all go on back there, I'm going through the house." I said as I ran inside. I tore open the manilla envelope. "Now will be a great time to see if this thing works."

I ran out back and met the others. Everything looked fine. But these animals aren't just going to start up over nothing. I held the necklace up and the sun glistened through it showing all of its purple tones. Nothing. The necklace didn't glow at all.

"Guess that was just a lie too," Henry scoffed. "That doesn't surprise me at all coming from him."

A large rock flew out from the wood line and landed with a hard thud near the cattle. Bigfoot!

That could be why the necklace didn't glow. Otis said it glowed when dog men were around. He didn't say anything about bigfoot at all. Maybe what he said wasn't a lie after all. I couldn't blame Henry for jumping to conclusions under the circumstances, however. Marie was stuck as tight to John's side as she could get. We tried so hard to see through the brush, but it was too thick. There may have been a slight shadow that was off from the others, but it was hard to say.

"I told you; animals don't belong out here," Henry said. "This is why. You guys are bringing in all kinds of critters by them being here. Now, it looks like bigfoot wants a sampler. Dog men don't throw rocks. That was definitely a bigfoot."

Just as he finished his sentence, he let out a loud, long whistle. Hearing whatever this was going back into the woods, allowed us all to relax. He once again looked at me with a smile and a wink. Maybe he thought he was communicating with them. No matter, it was gone now. It didn't make a difference as to why.

"What is that necklace that you brought out," Marie asked. "It looks similar to something that my mother always used to wear when I was a young girl."

We all turned to look at Marie. Could it be possible that her mother wore a necklace the same as this for the same reason? She had said that she experienced dog men at her house and saw one when her and her mother was hanging up clothes. Is it possible though is the question. It would be a stretch.

"This is a dog man necklace, Marie," Connie said taking it from my hands. "If you have this necklace with you or you're wearing it and a dog man is near, the purple stone will glow. It's really cool, isn't it? It's like a protection stone."

Marie took it from Connie and eyed the stone enveloped in the heavy metal ring. "Yes, this is exactly like the one my mom wore. I remember it perfectly now. She never really went anywhere without it, at home at least."

John turned to Marie. "You said you had seen one of these dog men at your house growing up. Once when you and your mom was doing laundry and then once again before you left for college. Did your mom happen to say anything to you at all about this?"

Marie thought for a while and said, "Well, no, she didn't. I knew the day we were hanging laundry to dry; she went inside and asked me to finish. When I left for college, she didn't come outside, but she was standing at the door inside waving at me as I pulled off."

John appeared that he was letting all of this run through his mind. I could see him questioning everything I was right then. Why would a mother leave her child out to finish laundry knowing there was a dog man around. Plus, she let her daughter leave and didn't join her outside before she left. Wouldn't a mom want their child to be safe over their own safety? I know Connie and I didn't have any children; however, I could only think that's how it is or how it should be.

"Any idea where your mom got that necklace, Marie?" Henry asked.

"No, I have no idea. I just know she'd always had it from as far back as I can remember. Are you guys thinking that she knew what the necklace meant and that's why she always wore it?" Marie asked.

"To me," John said, "It would make sense but why she wouldn't tell you about these dog men and had you find out on your own, isn't something I totally understand."

With all threats to our animals and property gone, we all went inside. A plan was what we needed so we all gathered in the living room to talk things through. I think at the end of the conversation, much to the girls' dismay, me and the guys all agreed that we should camp out. I had totally been against the idea of the whole thing at first, but if these things are gathering up here nearest to our house, maybe if we stayed near the second creek, we would be safer. Plus, we were now armed with more knowledge than we'd ever had along with a "detection" necklace, if it truly worked that is. If not, I always had the hulk hiding inside waiting to come out as long as Henry would be nearby.

"I actually think it would be smart if we get Ashton in on this and he and I stay near the cave where the bigfoot was throwing rocks at us, and you and Henry can stay there near the second creek."

Marie stormed off and stopped right before she bolted off out the door. "This is ridiculous, John, and you know it. If you want to go put yourself in danger with no regards to me, you go right ahead. You're a grown man and I don't control you, but I don't want to hear a damn word from you when you try to come to me crying about how close you came to dying out there."

The door slammed hard behind her, and she drove off in the truck throwing dust up behind her. I had a feeling that Ashton's wife would feel the same way Marie did, probably to a higher degree since Ashton has children. This isn't worth breaking up marriages over and honestly, this isn't technically their problem. It's mine and Connie's property, not theirs. I understand them wanting to help, but the toll it's beginning to take, maybe we should reconsider this plan.

"I tell you what, John, I'm going to take you home seeing as how Marie left in your truck. There has to be a different way this is handled. It's either going to have to be just me and Henry go or there will have to be a different plan altogether. I'm not breaking up homes for this.

I couldn't blame Marie. I knew how crazy doing that would be, but I for one, was tired of dealing with this and now, it's not just cryptids on our property we're dealing with, it's helping someone else other than ourselves. Henry is a good enough person to not want to leave us with this mess to deal with on our own. He doesn't have to stay, but he does. He wanted to clear us as well as himself, from this terrible curse that he unintentionally brought to our property.

TIFFANY S. DORAN

Connie, Henry, and I sat out on the back deck later that day surveying the woods where the rock flew from the trees and landed in front of us. We had to figure out something to do. All the work we had put in thus far would be useless if we didn't.

"How about, you two go into the woods. Take the necklace and everything you would normally take to camp. Mark, you're armed with whatever this is you feel when you're with Henry and the dogmen are around, and as I said, you have the necklace as well. I don't want you to put your lives in danger, but this is getting monotonous. Then, the rest of us, whomever wants to, can stay here at the house to be back up if you need help. It's the only way." Connie said.

Henry looked at me and smiled. "She has a point ya know, it's the only way and the only way that makes sense when you look at everything as a whole. You're currently the property owner and I am the previous owner who started this whole thing to begin with. We have to be the ones who put an end to it. Once and for all."

After talking to Marie, John was able to calm her down. The new plan was discussed and agreed upon. Henry and I would be the ones to go camping in the woods. The rest of the gang would set up at our house and keep an ear out. I was able to rent some equipment to take to help us navigate easier and I also rented a flir camera. It would allow us to see both of them if they happened to be lurking about. Henry and I walked into the woods and straight back to the second creek and set up camp. We had arrived there shortly before dusk, so the woods were still noisy with birds and other things scurrying about.

"Well, I reckon all we can do know is wait now. Once the sun goes down, that should be when the real fun begins. I know for a fact you and Connie hadn't stayed out here at night and Ashton hadn't ever spoken of it either. That would mean that no one has been out here since I was last," Henry said. That will spark their curiosity.

"I hate that we can't be in both places at one time," I told him. "But I think we're positioned in the best place for the dog men. The bigfoot are closest to the cave, not over here."

"Yeah, not too much to worry about with the bigfoot." Henry replied.

I had to take his word for it because the last run in we had almost ended in a concussion.

We stoked the fire again once the sun had finally set. With the flames and flying embers, more than likely any small animal would avoid this area leaving the only sounds to be ours and the dog men. Currently however, everything was quiet except the insect and frogs. Henry and I sat talking of many things that evening and it made me even more determined to help him. He was a genuine soul, and you don't find many of them around these days. He had a big heart and family meant more to him than anything. Now, what family he had left, wanted nothing to do with him. It was heartbreaking to hear him talk about. Then, silence fell across the whole are like a large hush was pushed through the trees.

Henry and I both looked at one another, barely taking a breath. We listened intently for anything, but it was so quiet that it almost hurt your ears. Just across the tops of the trees a short distance away, we heard a bigfoot whistle and then a tree knock in reply. I wonder what they say when they do that? Is it a location signal, are they saying they sense someone, or are they saying there's danger? I had always heard on the shows I listened to that the people in the woods would yell or knock on trees to see if the bigfoot would talk back to them but, do they really know what they're saying? I would have to say that it would be doubtful at best. No one really seemed to know too much about them.

"Showtime," Henry said with a smile. "Now we wait to see if those dang dogs come. The bigfoot sound as if they're still positioned near that old cave."

"Is that why you always sat nearest to the first creek, Henry, because the bigfoot were mostly there?" I asked.

He chuckled. "Yeah boy, I knew they wouldn't let anything get me. They would whistle and I would whistle. I felt that I were safe there. I hadn't ever had anything like what you and John experienced happen to me in that spot."

These were strange beings. It only further solidified that what we had happen was a one off with a rogue. Maybe when Henry did that incantation spell, it brought over more than what he bargained for or opened something he wasn't expecting. Then again, none of it was expected. It wasn't supposed to happen the way that it did to begin with.

"Do you reckon the bigfoot know about what you did Henry," I asked him. "You know, with the spell. You said the bigfoot were here first. Do you think they were able to sense what was happening?"

"I absolutely do, Mark. Bigfoot are a lot like us, in my opinion. There is something special about them though, different. They carry something we don't or can't. I don't know what that may be, however. But they were wielding these things away until I opened the whole gammit and they flooded the area. Now, I think there's a turf war. That's why you see the bigfoot near the cave where some of the dog men reside and the other dog men up here where we are."

I thought about that for a minute, and it dawned on me. "Henry are these the same dog men from the same pack. Dogs have different packs they are with most of the time. Do you think the dogmen in the cave are one pack and these up here, who seems to be more sinister, are ones from Otis's property?"

Henry was silent as he took that in. I was beginning to think that the idea never crossed his mind but to me, the answer was clear. If that were the case, and I'm leaning for it to be, the ones at the cave are the ones that have always been here and have to be easily controlled by bigfoot. If not, and they were all in the same pack, these up here would be in the cave as well. But they're not. In that case, the one I shot wasn't rogue, the one I shot was from Otis's property and therefore wouldn't be under the control of the bigfoot here at all.

"You're right Mark. I can't say that I ever thought of that, but that one hundred percent makes sense. That's the only way it could be. The dog men came from Otis's and probably tried to assert their dominance here and failed so they were separated and now, there's two packs. None of them good I might add but these are worse here." Henry said.

"You're right Mark. I can't say that I ever thought of that, but that one hundred percent makes sense. That's the only way it could be. The dog men came from Otis's and probably tried to assert their dominance here and failed so they were separated and now, there's two packs. None of them good I might add, but these could be far worse here." Henry said.

Just then, twigs began to snap and crack and the hairs on my neck as well as Henry's began to stand on end. I started to feel myself get angry. When Henry looked over at me, he knew. At that same moment, the necklace glowed a bright purple with every hue showing its shade. They were here, somewhere in the dense forest. But we couldn't tell which side they were on. He and I both stood up almost circling waiting for something to rush us through the tall vegetation. They're behavior seemed different this time though. The other times we were here, they were almost toying with us. Small growls here and there. This time, it's as if they knew we knew the secret. Their true whereabouts. These were vicious, snarling growls that came almost from the bottoms of their dog like feet all the way through their boisterous lungs and out through their mouth and snout. My mouth went dry and my heart raced.

"They're definitely here somewhere, Mark. Be ready. This is what I felt when I did that ritual. But I thought I was sending the ones here out not calling more in."

Suddenly the woods exploded with a sound I hadn't ever heard before. It was almost like a steam whistle and trees fell left and right straight in front of us. Henry and I jumped backwards but although fear ran rampant inside of us, we stood our ground. I thought for sure this would be our last night on earth. Everything floods your mind when that happens. I thought of Connie and our life together. How far we had come over the years as a couple. Our hunting trips together. I was glad that John hadn't come with us and especially Ashton. As the sounds grew closer to us, the necklace shone brighter and brighter.

Right before I felt we would meet our demise; the necklace began vibrating and it was as if the sound of a hum came from it. We could see the red glow coming from the sparse trees. There had to have been at least three of these creatures. I was in shock and was thrown right back to the night I shot that one. These looked the exact same way. As Henry held the necklace up, the stone spun in circles, still glowing its bright purple shades. Just then, a bright flash came from stone and the necklace grew dark once again. Henry and I stood gasping for air, fear still racing through our veins. There was silence. No more twigs snapping and cracking. The red eyes that felt like they were mere inches from our faces were gone, and everything had once again fallen still.

"I'm sorry, what in the hell just happened?" I asked Henry in bewilderment.

He looked just as confused as I did. He stood holding the necklace and looked around. The only noises you could hear were the pops and cracks from the fireplace, then the frogs started up again.

"I wonder if Otis knew it would do that," Henry said, eyes wide. "I doubt he did because if so, he wouldn't have gone in when it started to glow, he would've just stayed outside and let the necklace do what it does. That or, he did know but was too afraid to stay outside and see if it were true or not. Guess I can't blame that old man for that though."

I sighed a long sigh. "This just keeps getting weird. This is stranger than any fiction story I've ever read, Henry. He did say that an old medicine man gave it to him. Maybe he believed it only glowed as a warning but did nothing else because he didn't give it time to. If he went in after it started glowing, then you're right, he probably didn't know it would make them go away if they tried to attack."

He and I walked back and sat around the fire, both quiet for some time before we started talking again. We just listened to the sounds surrounding us. Crickets, frogs, and finally, the small little footsteps from smaller animals along the forest floor. After about an hour had past, I called Connie on the walkie. I wanted to let them know that we were okay, and I told her some of what had just happened. I told her I would tell her more in the morning, but that Henry and I were going to try to get some sleep.

"You just do what you have to, to come back home. Mark, I'm not kidding. Don't try to be some kind of hero out there, Connie said sternly. "John and I will be right here waiting just in case you need us."

I assured her that we would be fine. We set up some cameras along with the voice recorders and Henry and I crawled into the tent, leaving the campfire going. It felt like only a second had gone by and I heard noises like something walking outside of our tent. Heavy footfalls landed right next to my head. I was as still as could be. I heard small grunts that I was hoping would be picked up by the recorder we had set out. The necklace lay in between Henry and I and it wasn't glowing, this had to be a bigfoot. I sat up and saw that the campfire was still going just enough to cast shadows.

Yeah, definitely a bigfoot. The shadow that sprawled against the vinyl of our tent was large and you could see strands of hair hanging from this creature's arms. I didn't have a sense of fear, but I was curious. Henry had told me just enough about them for me to respect them but not to be afraid of them. I already knew from the other night what they were capable of. It milled around the campsite for a little bit and then I heard footsteps walking away.

Then a growl came out of nowhere. At that point, the stone illuminated once again. A lonesome howl broke out from the trees behind us. Henry woke with a start, and I quickly quieted him, so he didn't scream. Bigfoot yells surrounded us, and tree knocks could be heard from a distance. It sounded like a full-on vocal war. They were both preparing to fight, and Henry and I were stuck right in the middle of it with nowhere to go.

"What are we going to do, Mark?" Henry whispered as his voice quivered.

All I knew at that point is that we were absolutely stuck. This bigfoot had come up here and the dog men were angry that it was in their territory. Why had the bigfoot come up here anyway? I could only assume they were curious about us or maybe all the events that had just taken place. Either way, it was here, and I had a feeling that soon, they all would be. This would be amazing footage. It may also be the last footage we ever take, if it survived the brutal attacks that were about to take place at least it would be evidence for Connie as to what happened. I could only hope the recorders were picking every-thing up as well as the cameras.

The necklace was still glowing but not vibrating or making that hum sound. But I knew they were still around. An army of footfalls made their way to us, vibrating the ground with each step they took. Henry, still in his sleeping bag, sat in fear.

12

I couldn't blame him; I had no idea what the outcome would be. If any of these creatures fell on the tent, it would be like the weight of a small car falling on top of us. I went through everything we had in the tent with us to see what we could use for protection. We had two small knives, a machete, which would be useful, flashlights, and my weapon. We had some things to protect us but based off girth, and height, I doubted it would do anything to kill either of them. It would possibly at least cause enough harm for Henry and me to get away.

But, if there were more than a handful like it sounded, it still wouldn't do any good. It did at least bring us some sort of peace knowing we weren't unarmed. That's when I saw it laying off to the side. The walkie talkie. A direct connection to Connie and to John.

I quietly picked up the walkie amidst the howls of the dog men and the shrill screams of the bigfoot and called them.

"Connie, John, can you hear me?" I asked.

Silence that felt never ending loomed over us until finally a crackle came across. It was John and I was admittedly relieved it was him and not Connie.

"Hey bud, what's going on?" He asked.

"Listen, Henry and I are surrounded up here. We can explain

everything to yall later but right now, if we don't get some help, we won't have a later." I told him.

"What can I do to help, I'll do anything you need." He replied with a frantic tone.

A loud thud fell just to the far left of us. The glow from the campfire began to dim. Soon, we wouldn't only be surrounded by two hulking cryptids, but we would also be surrounded by complete darkness.

"John, I need a distraction. A good one. We have dog men and bigfoot up here right beside us and they're fighting. We have to get out of here but there will be no way unless you cause a distraction. We need them to move away from this area and come towards you so we can get out."

Henry and I began to pray. The call to arms had been made and once again, we could only wait to be saved. I just hoped it wasn't too late. The thud of bodies around us was intense. The noises both of the creatures made was unmatched to anything we had ever heard.

"I'm sorry, Mark. I'm sorry for all of this. This is all my doing and now you're in danger." Henry looked like he was going to break down at any second.

But all at one time, the woods echoed. This time, from a different sound and it caught us all off guard, including these beasts that continued to wrestle around just outside of our tent. Air horns rang through the trees, then three shotgun blasts. The sounds around us quieted as if they'd stop fighting to look at what may be coming. The bigfoot tore away first, clamoring down the mountain side, pushing trees over in the process. The dog men left second making loud howls and tearing branches as they ran away. Then, it was just me and Henry. We didn't dare move. The necklace no longer glowing, proved that at least the dog men were completely gone.

"What was that?" Henry asked, eyes opened wide.

I smiled. "That was the calvary."

I listened for a bit longer but once we had experienced nothing but the natural sounds of the woods again, I slowly and cautiously unzipped the tent. Looking around, it appeared to be a war zone. The table we had everything sat on was in half. I had no idea where any of our devices were and knew that finding them would be impossible until daylight. Loose tree branches and leaf litter lay everywhere. It was surprising that we had survived that. Anything could have been thrown and landed right on top of us. Henry crawled out of the tent and stood in awe at the sight of everything.

I grabbed the flashlights and the necklace from inside the tent, stomped out the remnants of the fire and we hightailed it out of there. When we got closer to our house, the woods were lit up like the noon of day. Two vehicles sat at the edge of the wood line and all three had their bright lights and hazard lights on. We were so relieved to be out of there. I hugged Connie as tightly as I could, and Henry went to John sobbing.

We sat in the kitchen at the table and went over every harrowing, scary account that had happened. It was all so surreal just saying it. It was as if I was telling a story of science fiction that I had written. There's no way that actually happened. But it did.

"Yeah, no way to explain the necklace glowing and then vibrating the closer to us they got. Much less, the bright flash and then having everything disappear like they weren't there in the first place." I said.

Henry took a long drink of the beer he had sitting in front of him. He was ragged and tired. He wore it openly on his face. You can't hide it once you experience it.

"Otis said that an old medicine man gave it to him. It was probably equipped with that, but again Otis was too much of a dunce to realize it. Like I told you in the woods, Mark, we wouldn't be in this mess now because he had a sure-fire way to make them vanish if they got too close."

"So, does that mean you don't actually have to break the curse then, Henry," Connie asked. "If that necklace makes them disappear if they get too close, then Mark and I just need to wear the necklace to go into the woods with you not here, right?"

Henry chuckled. "Would you want a blood curse on you if you had a way to make it go away?"

Connie sat back in her seat. "No, I guess you're right, I wouldn't."

It was a good thought and one that would probably work but this had to be dealt with so Henry could finally have peace from his past, peace from everything that had happened.

"We'll have to go back to get all of our gear when it's daylight. I would love to survey all the damage when we can actually see it. We need to gather all the cameras and such as well. I'm hoping that they're not destroyed, and they picked up at least some of this battle." I said.

"I'm just glad you two made it out of there." John said.

I laughed as I finished my beer. "Yeah, us too. Nice thinking on part of the air horns and shot guns. That had them all running for the hills. It gave us just enough time to get the heck out of dodge."

"Yep, you said you wanted a good distraction, and I would say that was good a distraction as any. No animal, no matter what it is, like loud noises like that. I figured too, if they came towards the house, that the bright lights would steer them away hopefully even further into the woods at that point."

We sat around for a little longer before we all went to bed. I was so exhausted that it felt like I was already asleep before we even made it into the bedroom. But we only slept a few hours before daylight woke me up pouring in through the window and the roosters started calling. I stumbled to the coffee pot and got showered and dressed. I would be so glad when this is all over and done with. I walked out and took care of our livestock and looked into the woods. It was still hard for me to believe that less than twelve hours prior, I was in the middle of a cryptid throwdown. I had said it before, how is this even our reality.

The others woke shortly after. John left to go home and get Marie and Henry woke up, fixed a cup of coffee and joined me out by the chickens. It was a peaceful morning. The small clucks from the chicken and sounds of rooting from the pigs was actually comforting. It all was. This was what I wanted our life to be. Surrounded by friends and living a peaceful life here on our little farm.

"You know," Henry said, "I will do anything I can to make this right. Not to be repetitive, but this isn't fair what you guys are having to deal with on account of me."

I looked over at him as he reached over to rub the back of one of our pigs. "I appreciate that Henry, I really do. I know you mean it too. Come hell or highwater, we'll sort this out."

Connie joined us shortly after. She was so beautiful in the light of the sun. I wanted more for her. She was my motivation in all of this. Even if we had to live with these devilish monsters, I just wanted to be with her. John and Marie showed up a few hours later and he had actually talked Marie into going into the woods with us. I was surprised because that was something she hadn't ever done or agreed to the whole time we'd been dealing with this.

"How in the hell did you pull that one off, John?" I asked surprised.

"I told her she could wear the necklace. She knows she will be safe with the necklace. Does hurt the ole ego though seeing as how she feels safer with a necklace then me but hey, I'll take it." He chuckled.

Marie was mesmerized by everything she was seeing. The first creek where John got their fish from, the whole expanse of the woods she saw from our first horrific run in, it was all so beautiful to her. But I knew under all of that, she was afraid just the same. She grabbed on to the necklace and rubbed the stone as she walked ahead. We finally made it back to where we had our harrowing experience. The only thing standing was our tent. There were small saplings that had been pushed down or thrown and leaf litter covered the ground.

The table we had was in pieces. I gathered all of the equipment we had taken out there and put it in a bag. Connie was silent. She really hadn't said too much since we got there, and she saw everything. I walked over to her and put my arms around her waist. She turned to face me, and I saw the tears in her eyes.

"I know," I said wiping them away. "I know.

We walked out of there after grabbing a few more items and headed back home. I couldn't wait to hear and see what we caught, if anything. I laid everything on the table in the dining room and I examined everything making sure nothing was cracked or completely broken. If it were, I would have to buy all of this. I laid the recorder out on the table and pressed play. We all gathered around it and stared at it intently. It was silent at first. I thought for sure it was busted but then it started playing. You could hear Henry and I as we zipped up the tent, our brief conversation, and then Henry's light snoring. Footsteps followed that, heavy footfalls.

"That must be when the bigfoot came to the camp!" I said excitedly.

Rustling and static filled the speaker just then. There was some electrical interference it sounded like.

"But what was up there that would cause that? I wondered.

"Are there any power lines out that way Henry?" I asked.

Henry was quiet as he sat thinking. "Well, only over at Otis's place. But none that would be in the woods, no, what are you thinking?

That made all the sense in the world. These dog men came from Otis's. There is a connection with bigfoot and power lines I had heard, but no one really ever knew what that connection could be. Just another question to be answered with a question. We continued listening and we all heard low toned growls. A shrill scream followed but then the recorder cut off. I fiddled with it trying to get it to play the rest, but it only got that first little bit of the beginning of the brawl. The camera only showed a dark shadow making its way through camp but then interference came in and it cut off as well.

Must be the electricity there too. Damn it. That could also explain why the flir was acting up. But it was all battery operated so I don't even know why the electricity would interfere. Of course, it did all have electric components. Either way, it was all useless with the exception for a few seconds from each device. The hair stood on both mine and Henry's arms just listening to that small clip. It put us both right back there again reliving everything. The table was quiet. No one said anything. I honestly think that they didn't know what to think or what to say. Even just those few seconds was enough to almost paint the picture of how bad it really was. The screams and roars were so loud, they vibrated our insides. This clip didn't do it justice.

"That must've been horrendous, guys," John said. "I'm shocked you even wanted to go back into the woods to get the equipment. 'You're right, I didn't but we really weren't given an option. This had to be done. You tuck your fear away and do what needs to be done." I said in reply.

We all went and sat outside and waited for Ashton and Sabrina. I had called them and wanted them to hear the recording as well. These creatures were brutal. There's no way that any weapon we had would take either one of them down. This was all part of the curse. I often thought of the one I shot in the face. Where did it go and how did it just vanish? Still being realistic, it couldn't have survived that shot.

Ashton showed up and told us that Sabrina had stayed home with the kids, but he came in and listened to the growl and the scream.

"Yeah, I heard that when we lived here. I always thought it was a bobcat or something fighting. Not so huh?" Ashton asked.

I laughed. "Couldn't be any further from the truth."

Ashton sighed. "Well, we all tell ourselves things to help us to be able to sleep at night. I guess that's what I did."

I get it. If I hadn't had seen it or been right there when they were both slinging their bodies around, I would've told myself the same thing. But I know the truth and now he does as well.

"Why do the powerlines matter?" Henry asked repeating the question.

"This is my theory. I can't claim this to be true however, the powerlines I had read about, were said to be good communication and hunting trails for bigfoot, along with railroad tracks. Even though no one knows for sure. So, what if it wasn't the dog men buzzing with electricity messing up the recordings but what if it were bigfoot? On the flip side, since these dog men came from Otis's side of the property, what if it were in fact the dog men who were harnessing some sort of power from the power lines?"

"They could both be plausible explanations for this," John said. "I read about that too. Have you thought about the fact that it could have been coming from both of them?"

"I haven't but it would be understandable. Maybe, the bigfoot that came into camp had just come from Otis's place hunting. These dog men had been cast out from there however, they may go over there from time to time, they just can't stay."

"So, they both came to our camp around the same time and boom. War." Henry said.

No matter what caused the fight. My goal was to never get caught in between them again. I think we needed to travel past the second creek to see if there's an entryway or an exit point either one of the creatures could be taking. Maybe we could get a better idea of their hunting and anything else. Now that I think of it, better than that, maybe Otis had written some of this down in all the paperwork we trudged through the other night. We were too tired that night to look at all of it. I got the manilla envelope and we spread the papers out on the table. Each one of us took a different stack and thumbed through it to see if we could find anything at all to explain what was going on.

I found in his chicken scratch, something that looked like it could possibly say that he had seen a bigfoot on his property, but the date was illegible. It does say that one of the dog men chased it away, but it didn't give any specifics as to which way this bigfoot ran. That would prove that the bigfoot going over there had been a common occurrence. At the time however, that was solely the dog man's territory because the curse hadn't been cast yet.

"Well, the fact still remains, no matter the coming and goings on of these cryptids, this curse has to be broken." John said.

"Yes," Henry said. "The quicker the better."

13

Henry was discouraged. It would come in waves, however. Sometimes, you could see the glimmer of hope in his eyes but then other times, times like this, he felt that his demise would be the only viable option.

"But what happens if we don't break the curse?" Marie asked.

Henry sighed. "If we don't break the curse, not only will all of this that we've done been for naught, but it also means that this evil pack of dog man will be here to stay...forever."

"It also means that Connie and I would have to sell our livestock and move," I said. "At that point, us being able to stay here wouldn't be an option. We're far too close to them."

No one at the table with us wanted that to happen. We have all become such good friends and generally, once you move, friends lose touch. We have too much vested in this friendship. I am also refusing to believe that in the end, the only way for this curse to be broken is for Henry to sacrifice himself to undo this.

"You said the way you cast this spell so to speak, was a fire, blood, and then what you said around the fire right," Connie asked. "To break it, without it being by giving up your life, what would you need?"

I had been researching this as soon as I found about the blood oath, what they actually entail, and what happens afterward. I, of course, found many people selling bogus ways to break them. Trying to make a buck off of the desperate. Despicable. But with Henry tweaking this so much for his boys, finding something to break the main curse would be key.

I was hoping that once we broke the main one, the other tweaks would just fall away and not matter. I decided to go to the library and look for what I could find to help. I found pages and pages of lore, cryptids, witches, and spells, both fiction and nonfiction alike. I didn't know exactly what I was looking for, so I walked to the front desk and asked the librarian.

She cast a sideway glance when I asked where I would find a book on how to break a blood oath. I would've done the same, honestly. It was a pretty blunt way of putting it. Nonetheless, I told her that I had looked at the books on the shelf but was unable to find anything. She grabbed a set of keys and told me to follow here. We walked to a door off to the side of the main library. She flipped the light on, and I was met with shelves of what I could only believe to be archives.

She told me to take my time and she walked away. I ran my finger along the spines of all the books. They were very old books, and they were all covered with dust. This was a room filled with answers, it had to be. I spent several hours in there and picked put a few books that hadn't carried their age well. Tattered pages, moth eaten, and brittle, but they held more answers I felt, than anything I had been able to find thus far. I walked them up to the counter to check out and thanked her for the time to search through them all. I called Henry to the kitchen when I got home and laid all the books out on the table.

"I found these in the archives at the library. They're fragile as you can see but these are books that may help you figure out how to reverse what you did all those years ago. You can finally be free."

Henry grabbed all the books, thanked me with the crooked smile of his, and took them out to the back deck to start looking through them. He came in only once to ask for a notebook and pen. Connie walked in shortly after asking where Henry was. He had almost become a fixture in our house now. We would all miss him when this was all over with. He's become a great friend. Later that night at dinner, Henry was telling us of all he had found in the books. He had painstakingly poured over every page of almost every book.

"Now look Connie," Henry said as he downed the last bit of tea in his glass, "I know you don't want any of this evil on the property and trust me, I don't either. But to try to reverse this, I have to go back to the same spot I first did it."

Connie sighed as she leaned back in her chair. "Well, where did you first do the ritual?"

"Right there in the clearing where I was sitting when you guys saw me on the trail camera." He replied.

Makes sense, I can only assume that would be why the large black one came there that night. Maybe it thought John and I were Henry. Boy did he ever get a surprise.

"Whatever you need to do, Henry, I'll support it for you. That will ensure all evil is off the property altogether." Connie smiled.

"Yes ma'am, for good hopefully." Henry said as he put his plate in the sink.

He gathered his books and went back to the living room and straight back to reading. Connie and I cleaned up the kitchen and went and sat on the deck. It was a star filled sky. Calm winds blew around us.

"Just think, Mark, pretty soon we will be able to do this all the time without fear." Connie said as she looked up at the sky.

I couldn't wait for that a moment longer. It had been pretty quiet since our adventure camping, but I knew they were there and that's what was the most disturbing for me. Probably Connie as well honestly. But we were doing our best and that was proving to work okay for us. But with everything gone, it would be a weight lifted from our shoulders for sure.

We both turned in and went to bed. Her words echoed in my ears as I lay there beside her. Being able to do that without fear. With all of this gone, we would be able to do a lot of things without fear again. Maybe we would even get a horse. I know we would plant more.

Being stuck inside and having it not safe to go too far from the house, was really proving to be difficult with planting and harvesting. We had some things, sure, but what we actually wanted to do would be more labor intensive. It certainly wouldn't bode well for our plans to have some demonic creature on the property at the same time. I was hoping Henry would find out what he needed to do with all the books I had brought home. He was certainly all into it and he had taken at least two to three pages of notes so far.

The next morning, we woke up and couldn't find Henry anywhere. He wasn't in the shower. We had checked the backyard and deck thinking he was out there reading. He wasn't on the front deck either. All of his books were actually inside at the foot of the sofa bed. I felt bad for this, but I went through his pages of notes. I was thinking maybe he had written Connie a note on where he was. He didn't.

"You don't think he went into the woods do you, Connie?" I asked frantically.

"Only one way to find out," she said. "Let's go out there before he turns into dog food."

I wrecked my brain trying to figure out why he would come out here all by himself knowing what he does. Does this have something to do with that stupid ritual he has to do? We got out of the truck and high tailed it into the woods. Sure enough, there he sat in the clearing. I could hear movement all around us. He heard us come up from behind and put two fingers to his lips to tell us to be quiet. Several knocks echoed out a few seconds later. Then a whoop in reply.

I tip toed over to Henry and sat beside him.

"What in the hell are you thinking coming out here alone?" I whispered in his ear.

He turned to me and smiled. "It's all going to be okay, Mark. I found out the answer. I know how to break the curse and set all of us free!"

Connie walked over and sat down with us. "Can we talk about whatever this is at home, somewhere that is safe, you guys. Now is not the time or place for a campfire story." She got up and walked to the truck leaving me and Henry sitting on the ground.

"I'm sorry yall, I just got so excited I wanted to go back to the clearing and get everything prepped. I wanted to let the bigfoot know that I was going to fix everything, and they wouldn't have to worry about the evil dog men ever again real soon."

"Next time, please leave a note." Connie said.

I sat down on the couch. "So, tell us Henry, what is this great plan to undo all of this?"

Henry excitedly sat down beside me. "Well, it has to be done on a full moon. There's no other time to do it in but then. Seeing as how these are partially wolves as well, they always are at their worst on a full moon, and they'll be clustered together then too. I will gather sticks just as I did all those years ago to make a campfire. As the full moon reaches its highest point in the sky, I will say what is in the book right there. Basically, casting them out of the land altogether. I just need a few more things."

"Whatever you need, we will help you with Henry." Connie said.

"You too, Mark?" Henry questioned.

I was taken aback by that because if Connie agrees to it then why wouldn't I?

"Of course, buddy. I figured you would know that already."

Henry sighed. "I had to ask you because you are going to play a pivotal role in this as the current landowner and I need your permission."

I didn't like the sound of that at all and I know Connie didn't either. We were all for helping Henry and ourselves but why would I have to give him permission to do that?

"I'm sorry, I don't quite understand why you need my permission to undo this. This is between you and whatever you made this oath with."

Henry looked timid and almost like he could crawl inside of himself.

"Well, it's because what I need from you personally, you have to willingly give me. That's why."

Connie sat down and looked Henry eye to eye. "What is it that you need from Mark?"

Henry looked like he wanted to cry. "There's no other way, Mark. For this to be broken at all, I need a part of you."

I was flabbergasted. "A part of me," I yelled sternly. "Why do you need a part of me, what part of me?"

Henry covered his face with his hands. "I need your... blood, Mark. Not much mind you, just a little."

As if that was going to make this okay. I'm supposed to willingly give this man a portion of my blood to use during a ritual. I couldn't take anymore. I had reached my limit. I was willing to help him do anything, but I couldn't have him use any part of me with this whole thing. I didn't want to chance it. This is dark magic, and I don't want my name, nor my blood, attached to it.

"Henry," Connie said, "There has to be another way, why Mark's blood?"

"I wish there were miss Connie," he replied rubbing his head. "But that's the only way I have found in those books."

"Well perhaps those books are wrong, Henry." I said as I paced.

Henry stood up and went out to the back deck and sat down leaving Connie and I to think.

14

I had no idea what to do. On one hand I could see why he needed to do it but on the other hand, this was totally irrational. What happened if what he found in that book wasn't even linked with this? What then? Then, I would be attached to it, whatever that may be. Poor Connie at that point was just pacing back and forth. She was thinking of a way around this, I just knew it. She's a critical thinker and everything has to be processed and prepared for her to feel safe doing it.

"Can we use chicken blood I wonder, or maybe some from the cows or pigs maybe?" Connie asked.

"I wouldn't have the slightest idea, honey. I don't know anything about this. That would be a question for Henry. I tell you what, you go talk to him and I'm going to call John. I would love his advice on this." I said as I got my cell and walked out to the front deck.

I sat down outside and dialed his number. Three rings later and John picked up. I told him everything. How I had went to the library and got books from the archive and how Henry had run off to the woods, and then, what Henry had just told me. I was sure glad to have him to call to bounce ideas off of. I don't know what I'd do if he weren't here.

"Wow, Mark, that's a tough spot to be in. Have you looked behind him to see if he's right about that? Maybe he's reading something wrong and it's all a misunderstanding."

"I haven't, he just now told me right before I called you. I just didn't know what I should do, if I should go through with it or not. Connie is outside asking Henry now to see if maybe he could use blood from one of the animals instead."

"I know you want to help him, but you also have to think ahead. If you helping him is going to be hurtful to you, then no, don't do it," John said. "I know you have a big heart, but you have to factor you as well as Connie into this too."

"Yeah, you're right. Well, I'm going to go out back and see if Connie has gotten anywhere with Henry. I'll keep you in the loop as to what's going on. I just know the decision can't be drawn out. It has to be done on a full moon as soon as it reaches the highest point in the sky."

"Ok, sounds good. I'll see what I can find out as well on my end and I'll get right back to you if I find anything at all."

I slid my phone back in my pocket and just sat there looking around at everything that Connie and I had been able to acquire since we moved. I wouldn't jeopardize this for anyone. As much as I hate to say it, even Henry.

I walked inside and straight to the back deck where Henry and Connie were at still talking. I slid the door closed and sat down.

"Mark, I know you may be upset with me and I'm sorry. I didn't really have a chance to explain. I knew I had upset you and Connie and at that time it was just best if I gave you two some time to think about everything. She had asked me if we could use blood from the animals and the answer is no. The answer is no because even though they reside here, they don't have a connection like you do. You are connected to me based on what you feel when the dog men come around and I'm here. The only way to break that is to destroy this curse."

Even though I understand it more and it does make more logical sense to me since he explained it, it was still risky at best. But now, I truly am almost obligated to do this or else I will be carrying this damn curse around for the rest of my life. I thought about it for the next little while taking everything into account and trying to factor in how things would be if I took part in this and then on the flip side, how things would be if I didn't.

"When is the next full moon supposed to be, Henry, do you know? Also, what all do you need to be able to do this?" I asked.

Henry pulled out his almanac and looked it up. "Says here the next full moon is Monday of next week. That gives us five days to get everything squared away."

"Good, that'll give me more time to think and Connie and I more time to talk about this. I've called John and filled him in on it as well. He's just doing some behind the scenes searching to make sure everything is on the up and up. With those books being as old as they are, he wants to make sure nothing had changed, and we both end up screwed."

"Sounds good to me." Henry said.

I tossed and turned all night. When I did fall asleep, I dreamed Henry and I were in the woods around a huge, blazing fire. A white mist floated vertically about the flames and Henry, and I were engulfed in some sort of star filled galaxy all our own, almost a protective barrier. Out of the flames came droves of dog men and they were instantly absorbed by the shadows of the forest. It was a long night and one I was glad to be done with as I sat and watched the sun come up above the horizon. Another day, Another chance. I walked out to check on the cows, pigs, and chickens. I longed to be in their place. They didn't have a care in the world. Just sleeping, eating, and messing. They didn't have to worry about anything. I knew I had to snap my mind out of this funk it was in. I just had to face this head on like a man. Wallowing in self-pity would do me or Connie any good.

I was confused at how quiet it had been. No activity. No sounds except for the actual sounds of nature. It was very odd and very off-putting knowing what is actually out there just beyond the water. It was then in the silence, that I made up my mind. I had to grit my teeth and bear it and I knew I would probably regret it.

"Henry," I called into the back door, "Would you mind coming out here with me for a minute? You can grab some coffee on your way out. I would like to have a chat with you please."

About fifteen minutes passed and I wasn't sure if he had heard me or not. As I was standing up to go inside and get him, he opened the door with coffee in hand.

"What's up, Mark, is everything ok?"

"Sure, everything is peachy. I have thought and thought about this, and I even dreamed about it when I was able to sleep last night. I would like to see the book that you found the answer to our conundrum in. I want to see it with my own eyes. I'm not saying I disbelieve you; I just need to see it for myself to have clarity about this. I also need some validation, if possible, that Connie is going to be okay through this. I know that may be a big ask but she is my life."

Henry stuck his hand out to shake mine then. He looked me in my eyes as a man.

"Connie is a strong woman, I don't worry about her through this, I worry about you. I'm asking a lot of trust out of you, and I appreciate all your hospitality towards me. Not only that, your help and kindness when it comes to this subject. I want you to know that I will do my absolute best to protect you at all costs and I even explained that to Connie when she was out here. What you guys have done for me will never be forgotten. I'll run in and get you everything I have. The book I found it in as well as the notebook with all my notes. If you have questions about anything, just ask me. I'm not going to keep secrets from you and Connie."

I appreciated his sincerity. As I had said before, he was one of the genuine ones. You just don't find many like him. He brought me his book and his notebook and left me to read and gather my thoughts. I read through all his notes and was thankful that his penmanship was far superior to that of Otis's. That's when I ran across what it was that Henry was telling Connie and I. The book read it almost as Henry had said it.

"To break any aforementioned curses of the current land, both the previous landowner and current landowner, must, in a vial, mix their

blood together and pour it into the fire. At the full moon, both must be holding the vial as the liquid is poured. It is then and only then, that the curse will be broken, and the land will be set straight. You must be careful though. This will open a whirlwind for evil. Every evil beast and creeping thing will be summoned that has ever laid foot on the property and will henceforth be sent back to where it belongs. Both human and non-human alike."

I read that passage over and over again, sorting through what it all meant. Henry was right. For this to work, it had to go down just as the book read. I put the book down and read Henry's notes attached to that section.

He wrote, "Ask Mark for blood, full moon, and please let this work for all our sakes."

I closed the notebook and sat there silently. This would be a lot for anyone to take in. I felt bad for Henry, for all of us actually, and I could only hope that this is what will indeed set our land straight and finally be everything that Connie and I had hoped for when we moved. I called Henry to come back out to the deck. He sheepishly came out and sat back down facing me. I sighed as he sat down and pushed the book as well as his notebook, back over to him. He was quiet and didn't say a word. What could he say though? He came here as the key to everything that had been going on but now, I was the key, the final key. Without me and my participation, the land, as well as Henry, would be lost, forever.

"I read the passage you bookmarked repeatedly and everything you told Connie and myself was correct. The only way to bring the land back to what it needs to be, is by carrying out this ritual. I don't have to like it, but I have to do it. According to that, this is the only way." I said.

"That's why I needed your permission. We both have to take part in this and if you weren't in agreement, I wouldn't even be able to do it. It would be pointless." Henry said.

I stood up to walk back inside. I needed to talk this over with Connie and explain to her that this is how it has to be. There's no other way around it and for us to have any normalcy in our lives again, in five days, we will be doing this ritual in the woods. It's now not just for Henry's sake, but ours as well.

"This is just ludicrous, Mark," Connie said in a frustrated tone as she paced the floor. "Had I known this would all take place, I would've never suggested we move here. I would've never had Henry stay here."

I walked over and put my hands on her shoulders to try to calm down her anxious mind.

"There's no way we could've known all this would take place when we were looking for our forever home back in the city. I believe this is our forever home, but with a nasty past that we have to clear up once and for all. This can be everything we've dreamed about and more. You are always the positive one and right now, I could really use some of that positivity." I said trying to reason with her.

She let her head fall into my chest, and she wrapped her arms around my waist. I knew what her fear was and to be honest, I feared that as well. We couldn't go based off assumptions. We could only go off certainty. With everything going on, it all fell in line with how the book read. It has to be this way whether we liked it or didn't. it couldn't be based off that of our opinions, John and Marie's, or Ashton and Sabrina's. It was our life that was in jeopardy here, so it had to be our decision. We did need to bring everyone in on what was going to take place, so we called them all over for dinner one night. Connie made a big elaborate spread and even included dessert.

"Wow," John said as he made his way into the dining room and looked at all the food. "This must be something bad you guys are trying to butter us up for with all this."

They each took their place at the table and once they had filled their plates, we began the discussion of what would transpire within the next few days. It wasn't going to be an easy conversation and John was partly right. We were trying to soften the blow with homemade biscuits, roast beef, sides, and chocolate satin pie. In all honesty, and unbeknownst to Connie, if something went sideways and I didn't make it out of this, I wanted this one last meal with all of us together. It would be a memory I would carry with me into the woods. I was trying to look on the bright side of things, but I knew I also had to be real at the same time. This was a darker magic we were messing with and generally, it doesn't turn out well. I brought out the book that I had checked out at the library from the archives. I went over the passage with them that were instructions on how to carry out the ritual. I watched as each of their faces soured at the mention of it.

"This is the only way, guys," I said. "I know this isn't ideal, but hell, has any of this been ideal? We've dealt with this for longer than any of us have wanted. Ashton and Sabrina moved because of it, Henry moved because of it, I will be damned if Connie I will be chased off of the same property for the same reason. It stops now and this is the way to see that it happens."

They were all quiet, even Connie. I knew their thoughts without them saying it. I felt the same way at first, but after reading the book and going back over everything we had dealt with, it all made sense and whether they were on board with it or not, we were doing it.

"I'm not in your shoes," John began. "This has to be your decision and your decision only. I'm not going to sit here and try to talk you out of it. You have made a very clear case as to why it has to happen. I just want you to be safe, that's all. You and I have become very good friends since you and Connie moved in, and I only want what's best for you. If this is what you see as best for you and your wife, then so be it."

I was surprised by John's reaction and lack of push back. He and Marie had both been dealing with this too, and this would also bode well for them and their property. The way I see it, it's a win-win. Ashton had offered almost the same sentiments. He and Sabrina really had no dog in this fight since they moved to the city limits to be closer to her parents to escape this. But we had grown to be friends with them through this whole ordeal. In a sense, even though it was for a shorter time, they were attached to this lore. My main concern was for my dear wife, Connie. She really hadn't said too much through dinner. She was taking in all of everyone's advice, and she was simply enjoying being around friends. They really are the glue that holds things together in times like this.

"Can we come over while this is happening," Marie asked. "I would really like to be here for Connie while you're in the woods. I know that she doesn't need to be alone no matter how strong and feisty she is."

Connie looked over at Marie and smiled and laid her hand on hers. "Thank you, Marie, that means a lot and you're right, I don't want to be alone while all of this is happening. I can't be in the woods, none of us can. It can only be Henry and Mark. Having someone here with me will be much appreciated. This is a big pill to swallow, and I would only be wearing a hole in the floor by pacing and think awful things."

I was thankful for our friends, albeit we were brought together in a strange way, but they were true friends, nonetheless. Who else would support any of this that had taken place? Not many.

"So, this takes place on a full moon, is that because that's generally when werewolves are said to come out?" Sabrina asked.

"I could only assume so," I said, "But you also hear a lot of how bad things take place on a full moon. Not only werewolves, but witches, hauntings, and the like. These aren't really werewolves though, Sabrina. These are a different entity altogether."

We finished up dinner and we all sat in the living room talking. We went over the plan of Henry and I going into the woods around dusk and getting everything ready for the ritual to take place. We had to wait until the full moon was at its highest point. We talked of protection while we were waiting. I had no doubt that these creatures would be lurking as most animals did on a full moon. I'm sure that they would also know what Henry and I would be setting up for. It may make them more vicious as well. This was going to happen, but we also had to be safe about it. If we were eaten, this would all be for naught, and the curse would carry on forever. Not to mention how it would affect Connie.

"Marie and I will be here around five that evening if that's okay," John said. "We can help you guys gear up at least and make sure you have everything you need and that you're not forgetting anything."

"I would appreciate that," I said. "I will be scatterbrained that day and the fact that it falls on a Monday doesn't make it any better. Monday's generally suck anyway."

Henry laughed at that. "Believe it or not, Mark, the last time I did this fell on a Monday as well, and I can concur, that it didn't turn out to be a good day."

I appreciated the slight light-hearted turn this conversation had taken. It made the room feel more relaxed. I knew that our friends would do their best to be there for us.

Connie and I sat out on the back deck that evening after everyone had left. She had a glass of wine, and I had a beer. She didn't drink often so I knew she was stressed. It was quiet with only the sounds of our animals milling around, and the sky was full of stars.

"I would say that was a successful dinner." Connie said smiling.

"Yes, I would agree. It was really nice sitting around with our close group of friends sharing the evening together. When this is all over, we'll be able to do that more often and not because we're trying to butter them up." I laughed.

'You're really going to do this, aren't you?" Connie asked as she sat her wine glass down.

"Of course, honey, I have to. There's no way around it. I'm doing this not only for you or me, but I'm also doing this for us, for our life here together. For better or for worse was the vow I made to you, and I plan on keeping it. The better will come soon enough...no matter what it takes."

15

The day drew nearer and nearer. I wrote out a letter for Connie to find later on if something went south. I made sure all of my affairs were in order as much as I could so that she wouldn't have to worry about them. Henry and I had talked one night of him doing the same, but he said he really didn't have too much to get into order. He didn't have a home, car, or anything that would really be in jeopardy if he didn't survive. I was still saddened by that for him. In essence, he didn't have anything to lose while doing this. He only stood the chance to be free from the bondage of this curse. I, on the other hand, had a lot to lose, which is why my decision to do this was more difficult than his.

Sunday morning, I sat out on the deck drinking coffee and watching the sun rise. It was my favorite thing to do and what brought me my greatest sense of peace. The lawn had been freshly mowed the day before and it glistened with drops of dew that sparkled as the sun's rays finally touched them. I thought of how beautiful this would look in the wintertime with freshly fallen snow kissing the ground. Maybe, Ashton and Sabrina could bring their children the next time since this would all be over by then.

I could almost envision them playing in the backyard, petting the cows, and giggling at the pigs rolling around in the mud. Everyone would be safe. Finally. Just as I was thinking how fun it would be to finally get to fishing with everyone, the back door opened, and Connie walked out in her housecoat carrying a cup of coffee. She was so beautiful. My motivation had always been her. This wasn't any different.

"How did you sleep?" I asked as she sat down.

She stretched and yawned. "Surprisingly well. I think just talking about everything and getting everything out into the open last night, helped put my mind at ease. I'm a planner, you know that, so formulating a plan was good for me. It made things feel structured. I'm all about structure." She said.

I knew that from the get-go when she and I first got together. I found myself reminiscing a lot about that recently. I was hoping for the best, but preparing for the worst, I guess. I wanted to hold on to as much as I could. I was very apprehensive about this whole thing. I had accepted all of it finally, but that didn't mean I wasn't still worried and even scared. I hadn't ever done anything like this, nor did I think I ever would. It's not every day that you live near the woods that are full of actual beasts trying to kill you. Much less, having to do a reversal spell using your own blood to make them go away. I wondered what my grandpa would think of all this. I was sure he hadn't ever heard of such a thing. But, like I said before, if dog men did live on their property, I never heard of it, and they were probably noted to be werewolves instead. They did carry some of the same characteristics, admittedly, but they were very different at the same time.

He would probably tell me I had lost my mind, and oh my goodness, grandma was probably rolling over in her grave to everything I was taking part in. I could see her now shaking her bony finger in my face telling me how I was going to get myself killed doing all this. Truth is, she may be right.

I shook that thought from the cobwebs of my mind. I had to think positive. If not, the negativity would overshadow all of the good that could come from this. Freedom, not only for Henry but for all of us. I had to harness the good thoughts and expel the bad. I spent the rest of the day trying to do just that. I enjoyed the day harvesting vegetables from the garden with Connie, feeding the animals, prepping and having dinner as we sat on the front deck. The evening had turned out to be just as beautiful as the day had been. Once darkness crept in and the porch light clicked on, the air suddenly felt different. It felt heavier than it had in a while.

"The full moon is approaching, Mark. I think that's what is causing the turn. Even the tides respond to the moon. I feel it and I know you do as well."

She was right. I felt it and I think it was heavier on me than her to be honest. The time was approaching to meet these dog men in the woods and attempt to be victorious. We would give it our best shot. I woke up early the next morning. Doomsday. I was groggy and tired from the night before. To be fair, I was slightly hungover. I should've stopped after Connie told me to, but I didn't. She had two glasses of wine; I had a six pack. I took a long shower to try to wake up and shake this hangover. I had to be the best version of myself today and that wouldn't be possible while hungover.

I chugged a couple cups of black coffee and took some Tylenol. Soon after, I started feeling better. Henry and I sat out on the back deck going over all the plans. We read as much of that book together as we could stomach. It wasn't my normal read and a lot of it was just plain boring to me. I learned a lot however, so that did play in my favor. Our phones seemed to ring off the hook between John, Marie, Ashton, and then Sabrina. I didn't fault them, however. They were concerned for our safety and were making sure we had what we needed. I don't think we could be any more prepared than what we already were. Now, the only thing we had to do was wait. I think that's the worst part of all of this.

The waiting, wondering, planning, then the most detrimental of all, thinking. We are our own worst enemy when it comes to fear. Most times, if we can get out of our own heads, we would see that the old adage is true, the only thing you have to fear, is fear itself. Of course, that would be easier said than done. Especially in this situation. Connie had fixed a late lunch, but I just wasn't hungry. I did try to eat something, though. I just couldn't finish it.

My nerves were starting to get the best of me as I watched the time tick away on the grandfather's clock sitting in the living room. The sound of the secondhand seemed to echo through the house. I partly wanted it to just be time already. I think it would be less grueling that way. Then all of this weight would be lifted, and we could finally put all the bullshit behind us and just be able to live. As the sun grew closer to setting, the more adrenaline Henry and I had streaming through our veins. John and Marie showed up at five on the nose, signaling that it was almost time. Ashton and Sabrina showed up shortly after.

"Here are the walkies, guys. Make sure they're on and turned to full volume," I said as I laid them on the table. If we get into a bind, we will yell for help and we need you all to be ready. Marie, Sabrina, I'm not going to ask you to come in the woods. But if something happens, I want at least two cars at the edge of the wood line and I want the lights on at their brightest settings and I want you to lay on the horn."

"What would you have us do?" Connie asked.

I thought about that one because I didn't want Connie in the woods either. It would be far too dangerous. I wanted her protected above anyone else.

"Connie, this may not be the most popular answer for you, but why don't you be the third car at the wood line with Marie and Sabrina. That way we have three cars' lights, three horns blaring, and if need be, take some more of the air horns we have."

Her eyes bore a hole into my soul. I knew she wouldn't be happy with that, but that's how it was going to be. She knew that, though. She didn't come back at me with any kind of rebuttal, surprisingly.

"John and Ashton, we need you ready. Bring your rifles and air horns. They seem to hate loud sounds. We found that out the night we went camping. They scattered like roaches after you turn on the lights."

They agreed and Henry left the room. We could hear him

rummaging through a bag in the living room. He came back in carrying a small vial. His hands had begun to shake. I could see it as he held the vial in between his thumb and forefinger. I walked over to him and tried to calm him as much as I could.

"We're in this together, Henry. You have my back and I have yours. This will all be fine. The main enemy we have right now are our own thoughts and time. Once we get out there, the buildup to all of this will be coming to an end." I said.

Tears welled up in Henry's eyes. "I can't say if I'm more afraid or more excited. I've carried this for a long time, and I have suffered a lot of loss because of it. Once we do this, I'll be free, we all will be. It's just the fact of going out there and getting it done."

"What is the vial for?" Sabrina asked.

"Their blood," Ashton answered. "Remember at dinner the other night, that's the biggest part of it. They have to mix Mark and Henry's blood together and both pour it into the fire."

It became all too real when Henry brought the vial into the kitchen. The thought of cutting my finger in order to add blood to the vial was frightening. We wouldn't do that here, however. That would be done once we crested the wood line and made it to the clearing of dirt.

"Are yall about ready? Connie asked.

Truthfully, no, I wasn't, not anymore. But the time had come. I kissed Connie long and hard before we geared up. I went back over all the instructions and then Henry and I walked the two miles to the wood line. The trees almost bent down to greet us and welcome us in. It was quiet. Only the slightest sounds of crickets chirping faintly filled the air. The woods had an unusual feel to them, and the air was almost heavy around us. Two tree knocks echoed around us.

"The bigfoot knows we're here." Henry said, once again smiling his crooked smile.

"Do they know what we're going to do ya think?" I asked.

"That's hard to say, it's possible, but those two knocks are letting others know that there are two of us here." Henry replied.

We made it to the clearing as night was almost upon us. Henry took the vial out of the bag, and I got out my knife. This was absolutely crazy. I tried to put myself back to when I was a boy. We would all make those blood brother pacts back then. The problem was, they never really stuck. Life happened and we all moved away from one another. None of us really spoke after high school. But this that I was getting ready to do with Henry, would be the strongest blood brother pact ever made anywhere. We positioned the vial between two rocks to hold it steady so it wouldn't fall over. Henry held out his hand.

"I just need your finger, Henry. I'm not slicing your hand open. You said we only needed a little bit." I said sternly.

Henry chuckled. "Yeah, I guess you're right, I just want to have enough."

"We will, I promise. I'm not letting a small error in calculation screw us out of this. We put too much into this." I said.

I held his finger as steady as I could. I didn't want to filet it open to where he would need stitches. Goodness knows we'd have to lie about how the injury happened or we'd both end up in the looney bin. I just needed enough.

"Turn your head, Henry." I said as I held up the knife.

Henry stood as still as possible, but he was already tightening up every muscle in his body and squinting his eyes. I came down fast with the tip of the knife right into the pad of his middle finger. He let out a yell as blood oozed from his fingertip. He held it over the vial and squeezed as hard as he could to get enough out. Good thing for us, Henry was a good bleeder. There would be plenty there. Now, it was my turn. I must admit though, I wasn't looking forward to this at all. Of course, I don't know anyone in their right mind who would be. I gave Henry my hand, turned my head, and waited for the pain as the sharpened knife came down. I tried hard not to yell, but it escaped my lips anyway.

I held my finger over the vial and did the same thing Henry did. Just then, as the blood came together, it started reacting to the mixture of my blood and Henry's blood. I held it up in the air as I put the cap on it. At this point, it was almost starting to shimmer. When I tipped the bottle slowly back and forth to fully combine it together, it was like that of a thunderstorm with streaks of what I could only say to be electricity going through it.

Henry looked as shocked as I did at the transformation. Needless to say, we had both contributed enough blood.

"What's it doing, Henry?" I asked as I looked at the swirling streaks of electricity running through it.

Henry took the bottle from me and looked intently at it.

"The reaction it's giving off is only proof that what we're doing so far is right. We've followed what the book said and we're on the right track." He smiled.

Now, we just needed to get the rest of the things in place. Henry and I gathered enough sticks to make a fire. Once it was built up to have a continuous burn, we just had to wait until the right time. Henry pulled the book out of his bag and we both sat down to look over everything to make sure the next steps were done correctly. The moon had started to rise and there was a cacophony of noises that began around us. It's almost like the creatures of the woods knew what was about to take place.

"It says here, we have to both hold the vial as we pour the blood into the fire." Henry said.

"Yeah, I remember reading that part, so I'm assuming then after that's done, we just stand back and let it do it's thing?" I asked unsure of how all this would play out.

Henry flipped through more pages and then pulled out his notebook. I was growing nervous with his behavior. He was searching through both of them like there was supposed to be more to it and he either forgot what that was, or it was missing. I didn't like how frantic his behavior had gotten.

"Bingo," Henry said loudly. "There it is, I was looking for the incantation to say. It's not enough to just have a fire and our blood, but we have to say what it is that needs to be done."

I looked at him confused. I didn't think what we needed to say was in that book based off of our specific situation. So, what are we supposed to do then, just make up some silly rhyme and call it out into the sky? If I hadn't been so far into this and knew it was real, I would walk away.

"I know, I know," Henry said sensing my disdain. "I had to do this when I did it. I threw in the specifications that I needed and wanted to have happen. The incantation was right and everything else was extra directed towards my family. That's why the dog men came but, the boys had a sense of when danger would be near. It was all jumbled together. This will be different. The incantation in the book is exactly what we need to send them away."

"But didn't you read an incantation out of a book before, and it turned out to be wrong?" I asked concerned.

"Otis gave me what I read written on a piece of paper. I didn't know any better and was far too desperate at that time, to ask questions. He wrote down what he wanted me to say, taking full advantage of me and the situation. The one in this book, is to send all evil away. Though it's not directly specified toward the dog men in general, they are evil so they would fall into this category. Actually, anything evil on this property at any time, past or present, will be brought here and cast away according to the book."

I thought about that and wondered how far back it would go to cast the evil of this property out. How many years? Would we have all evil creatures and all evil people from as far back as time began floating through here? This was so confusing but we're too far in to change our minds now. The only thing we can do is wait and see what actually happened. As we sat and waited, the walkie cued up.

"John here, just checking in on you guys, anything going on yet" he asked.

I reached over and grabbed the walkie off the rock. "Well, we gathered everything for the fire, just waiting for the right time to start it. Henry and I have already mixed our blood in the vial, and we've been going over the instructions in the book. How are yall holding up there?"

"Well, you know the girls are on pins and needles. We're just waiting on the word from you guys on what to do now." He replied.

"Just stay close to the walkie. We will be lighting the fire soon and getting everything in place. As the old saying goes, no news is good news. If you don't hear from us for a while, don't automatically think the worse, okay? If this goes down like I'm thinking it will, you will all know when the deed is done."

At eleven forty-five, Henry and I said a prayer for protection and lit the fire. It roared loudly as it sparked to life. The heat that emanated from it was as intense as this moment had become and we couldn't shake the fear that had started to grow within both of us. Henry and I looked at each other as if to say good luck and we hope to be on the other side of this. I hoped this would be the end of all the may lay of drama and lore, and we could both finally have peace. I hoped that more so for Henry than myself. This would be the end of almost a lifetime of loss, stress, and heartbreak for him. Henry walked over and pulled the blood vial from in between the two rocks that it was being held by. We both walked the fire and held the vial hand in hand. The full moon had then reached its highest point and it was finally time.

"Are you ready, Henry?" I asked smiling.

"Ready as I'll ever be, Mark. Thank you for everything. I'll be indebted to you forever."

"No, you won't. You've been in debt to this for long enough. You're going to be free."

We popped the top off the vial, held it up into the air, and slowly poured it drop by drop as the book said, into the flames.

16

As we poured the blood on the fire, Henry began saying the incantation he had memorized.

"On this land from times before, break this land from all its lore. From evil beast to evil souls, make this land, once again whole. To the things of the past, to the things that we see, gather them up and set us free. Cast them as far, as the east from the west, so this land can breathe and finally rest. No more shall we suffer or live in fear, bend down to see us and tell us you hear, our fateful cry we say tonight, to put an end to this all and finish this fight."

After Henry spoke those words and the last of our blood had been poured on the fire, everything went quiet. The fire weakened and almost completely fizzled out. Henry and I just looked at each other disappointed. I didn't know what to say. Why didn't this work? Maybe we had used too much blood, maybe not enough. Maybe, the moon had risen too much. Either way, we were deflated and felt as if we had failed. Henry looked like he was going to cry. I honestly felt like I was going to as well. We had worked so hard for this. It seemed to be all for nothing now.

"Well, we tried, buddy." I said as I patted him on the back.

Henry was silent. I walked over to grab the walkie to let everyone back at home know what had happened or didn't happen rather. But just as I did, Henry yelled for me.

"Mark, Mark, the fire!" he yelled.

I turned around and saw the flames rekindling and growing larger than it had been when we first lit it. Grey clouds covered the sky and almost overshadowed the moon as lightning streaked across the midnight sky. The winds began to blow hard against the trees, and we watched them sway ferociously from right to left as their leaves fell from the branches all around us. Henry and I clutched onto each other as we took in all that was beginning to happen around us, so much so, that we almost didn't notice that above the fire, a small ball of iridescent light had begun to grow. It sparkled and made a sizzling sound as if electricity was fueling it. It grew larger and larger until it was almost like a door opening.

Just then, awful snarling and growling echoed all around us. Henry and I were terrified and almost regretted what we had done.

"Is this normal, Henry," I yelled as the winds continued screaming. "Did this happen last time?"

Henry just looked at me wide eyed. "No, it didn't, he yelled back, but remember, the incantation I did before was to bring them in, they were already on Otis's land, they just had to cross over to here. I wasn't banishing them as I thought. Now we're banishing them, so this is probably supposed to happen."

I hoped so any way. It sounded as if the whole forest was being sucked into this portal.

"We got heavy winds here at the house," Connie said over the walkie. "A tree is down in the backyard and the animals are going berserk out there!"

Her transmission fell on deaf ears. The walkie was laying on the rock and we didn't hear anything except growling and snarling along with the screaming winds and trees breaking all around us. Everything was being sucked into the portal. Tree knocks began and we could hear the calls and whoops from all the bigfoot then. The woods were making their own groaning noises as the evil was being sucked out and it was the loudest, scariest thing we had ever heard.

We witnessed whisps of humanoid shapes floating through the air all around us and being pulled into the portal.

"Spirits," Henry yelled. "Those are the evil spirits of these woods!"

"Dog men spirits?" I yelled back.

"Ghosts, Mark. Those are what people consider ghosts from times of the past and time of the present."

Just then, dark shadowy figures flew by and were almost ushered in by the winds into this portal. I must admit, although terrifying and greatly trauma inducing, I was overjoyed that the incantation seemed to be working out as it was supposed to. But I was waiting for the beasts who had been harassing us and causing the most conflict, dog men. Roars like those never heard before and deeper than any lions growl were quickly coming our way. I was too afraid to grab my weapon but, what good would it do anyway? Henry and I looked around and he held up a shaking finger and pointed to just above the trees. It was the first of many dog men, but not in physical form, this thing came by us in spiritual form. We could both tell what it was all the same. The eyes were glowing red, and the fur was black as coal. Menacing teeth and pointed ears; everything we saw headed our way the night we went camping.

Henry smiled his crooked smile as he looked up at me. Each time one of these beasts got sucked into the portal we celebrated. As each evil spirit went into the portal, I was feeling more and more at ease and more confident that this would all be over soon. This was certainly the right incantation that we had done.

"Where are the spirits of the bigfoot," I asked as each evil, howling spirit went into the portal one by one over our heads. "Why haven't we seen them yet?"

Henry laughed as the wind blew what hair he had left all around his face. "Because they're not evil, Mark. They're only territorial. Their aggression doesn't come from evil. It's a natural emotion and a natural way of animals. They were here before we were. We have encroached on their land and for their family's sake, they are only protecting what they have left that we humans hadn't had the chance to overtake yet."

I never really thought about that, but some of the encounters I had listened to were downright terrifying. How could something like that not be evil? Who knows, I am not as versed as Henry. He could be absolutely right.

At that moment, something even more terrifying than any dog men appeared right before our eyes. Something we had only seen happen in movies. Off to our left, something began to flick in and out of existence right before our eyes before it was fully formed. It almost seemed as if it were a hologram at first, but we then realized that it too, was a spirit. Henry and I looked at one another in amazement.

"Otis," Henry yelled out. "How are you here, why are you here?"

I felt lightheaded and faint at that point. How was this possible? Otis was supposed to be at Shady Lakes retirement home. He was in a wheelchair when we saw him last but now, he was standing up face to face with Henry and I.

"You cracked the code I see you old coot," Otis said pointing to the portal above the roaring flames. "This won't be over until everything you said comes to fruition. That includes me."

"I asked for all evil from past to present to be drawn in and cast out, I didn't say you." Henry said.

"Who said I wasn't evil, Henry? You? How could you possibly know that. You know what I did to you, and I did it on purpose. But I knew then, that even though I did that to you, it was still too late for me."

He opened his shirt and exposed three large claw marks that streaked across his chest. They were glowing a red, ember color. He was marked by these beasts. I didn't even know what to say.

"So, you did that to me for no reason," Henry began. "Everything I went through was by your own doing and it wasn't even necessary. For what purpose, Otis, your own selfish gain?"

Otis laughed an evil, menacing laugh. "Of course, I had been marked. I used the necklace to let me know they were near so they couldn't pull me any further into the pack, but the damage had been done. I started acting out on my impulses that dog men carry, and that's why my ungrateful kids threw me into that home. They auctioned my land and rid themselves of everything they knew. Except for my money of course. You were just a pawn in my game of chess."

Henry let go of me and walked up to Otis's flickering image that had been going in and out. Sometimes he was a solid figure and sometimes he was a spirit. It was mind numbing to watch.

Henry spit in his face and laughed his own cackling laugh. Henry waited for just the right time when Otis was tangible once again. He laid his hands on his shoulders and said, "Well, check mate, you dirty bastard."

With that, and when Otis had gone to spirit form again, Henry flung him into the air and right through the opening to the portal. Otis screaming the whole way. Once Otis had disappeared into the portal, the ground began to shake, and the winds picked up again. A bright white light spread over everything in sight and the sky was almost as bright as the noon of day.

"Earthquake guys," John yelled over the walkie talkie. "Please come in, what in the hell is going on out there? Are you guys okay; please tell me you see that it's glowing white outside."

As soon as the white light had touched everything in sight, the woods fell silent. The winds, the shaking of the ground, The bigfoot yells and whoops. A large hush just seemed to have fallen over the property. The portal dissolved into itself, and the fire was then just a pile of embers and ash.

"Is it over, Henry?" I asked as I loosened the grip on him that I had once regained as soon as the ground started shaking.

Henry walked around the fire and then looked all around where we stood. Off in the distance, the sound of crickets and frogs could be heard. The sky was black once again and the stars seemed to be shining brighter than they ever had before. He squatted down and put his head in his hands and cried. I walked over and knelt down to wrap my arms around him.

"It's over," Henry cried. "It's finally over. I feel so weightless and free, Mark. I haven't felt like this in many, many years."

He stood up and hugged me sobbing.

"Hello," Connie yelled over the walkie. "You guys have to get better at your communication. What is going on? Everything just stopped here."

Henry and I laughed. While he went to gather up the bags that we had brought, I walked over to the rock that the walkie was laying on.

"We hear you guys loud and clear. It's all over and boy do we have some things to talk about when we get home!"

Henry and I, both tired, beaten down, and disheveled, made the two mile walk home. John offered to come and get us, but we needed time to process everything that had happened. It was all so surreal. We didn't feel an ounce of fear as we walked out the woods and we weren't afraid to walk home. It was truly over. We made it home and was greeted as soldiers making it home from war. Connie cried as she hugged me. Henry was crying again but tears of happiness as Marie and John hugged him. Ashton shook my hand and told me again how glad he was that he sold the property. The room erupted in laughter. We grabbed some snacks and drinks and sat down at the table in the kitchen.

We told them what had happened from beginning to terrifying end. I felt like I was reading from a storybook when I was telling them. It didn't even seem like it should be real life. It was too fantastical. Connie was as excited as a child at Christmas at the thought of being able to return to hunting, hiking, and fishing. I had thoughts already brewing for the garden. It was like being brought back to life again. I could only say that Henry felt more alive than we did. But that brought a thought to my mind. What will Henry do now, where will he go? He doesn't have anyone but us. We can't turn our backs on him and put him onto the street. Henry was family now. We were all up until around four that morning. Henry and I had so much adrenaline, there wouldn't have been anyway we could've gone to sleep any earlier. Finally, though, our adrenaline crashed and so did we. I slept until around ten the next morning and when I walked out of the bedroom, it looked like a frat party had taken place. Chip bags and soda cans were lying everywhere. John and Marie had fallen asleep in the recliners, Henry was in a ball on the couch, and Ashton and

Sabrina were on the floor for some reason. I just laughed and went to make some coffee.

I sat out on the back deck after feeding and watering our animals and took in the peace that surrounded our home and our property now. I was so hopeful for our future here. Amidst everything that had gone on. I wouldn't take a thing back. All the friendships that were formed wouldn't be as strong as they are now, had it not happened that way. Connie walked out shortly after. She sat silently as she drank her coffee, but I knew she was thinking and feeling the same way I was. The sun was warm on our faces.

"You know, the tree that fell last night can be chopped up for firewood. We can set all of that up now like we had planned. We can do everything we had planned."

She and I walked out across the expanse of our back lot and came up with all kinds of ideas to do now. We were no longer hindered by anything. This was ours to do what we saw fit. We heard the backdoor slam and turned around. Everyone was on the back deck now and walking our way.

"Seems like you may need some instructions on growing corn, there Mark." John laughed.

I nodded in agreement as I took a sip of my coffee. "Yeah, looks like we can do everything we had all planned shortly after Connie and I moved in. I would enjoy having the help."

"I'd be happy to help Connie and Marie plant some things too." Sabrina said smiling.

"She has a killer green thumb," Ashton spoke up. "I can help with any building projects you may have as well."

Henry stood off to the side silent, just taking everything in. The friendship and the sunshine.

"You don't think you're going to get off the hook that easy do you, Henry?" I asked as I nudged him.

Henry shrugged and drank his coffee. "I figured I should be getting out of yalls hair here soon," he said. "I have been here long enough and brought a load of things with me."

John walked over to him and reassuringly reminded him that it was over. He didn't have to carry the weight of something that no longer exists. I guess it is harder on him though. That was something he had carried for a long time so it may take longer for him to accept the fact that it's over more so than any of us.

"You are family now, Henry," Connie said as she walked over and rubbed his arm. "You aren't in our way, and we'd miss you if you left."

"I just don't want to impose. I feel like I have been quite the imposition already." He said in reply.

I understood and normally, one wouldn't just take someone in from the streets who claims to have a curse attached to them with dog men and a horrid past. But, I'm glad we did and there wouldn't be any way we could or would, send him back to the life he once knew. He finally had a fresh start. Even though we weren't technically blood related, we were in a sense now blood brothers.

"You know," John spoke up, I could always use someone to help me on my farm too. I have a lot of land and a lot of animals that need tending to. Would you be interested? I hear the owner pays pretty well." He finished with a wink.

"Of course," Marie said. "That way you wouldn't feel like you were imposing because then you could pay Mark and Connie a little to stay here."

"I hear the owners are really cheap on their rent too." Connie winked as she nudged him with her elbow.

It was then settled. Henry would live with me and Connie. I was glad he finally decided to do that. We all enjoyed our time fishing and hunting. Henry wasn't big on hiking, so he always went to John and Marie's instead. Ashton and Sabrina finally felt comfortable bringing their children over to play and Connie and I had bought them their own sand box and swing set. The winter was just as fun as I had imagined.

We added a fire pit in the back yard as well as a gazebo. We all sat around the fire pit and roasted marshmallows while the children made snow angels and built snowmen in the yard. Going in where it was warm and having hot cocoa was my most favorite part, however. I think about how everything transpired from time to time. How all the pieces came together to make our own family's puzzle. All pieces from different boxes that all fit together as they should. Sometimes, I think I should thank the dog men. They did bring us together. But then I think better of that. The bigfoot were still here and we would hear them from time to time. Calls made into woods and Henry still whistled at them. He knew now however, that he didn't need that whistle for protection. He used it as form of communication. The kids loved hearing all of the bigfoot stories Henry would tell them in front of the fireplace.

All in all, Dog man may have been a terror in our woods, but there would always be a means to an end. I must say, as I sit watching all of our friends that had now turned into family, that we had a pretty good ending.

AFTERWORD

Go to hangar1publishing.com to learn more about the Authors and stay up to date with their newest releases.

www.ingramcontent.com/pod-product-compliance
Lightning Source LLC
Chambersburg PA
CBHW071152120626
46546CB00006B/2226

*9 7 8 1 9 5 5 4 7 1 9 0 9 *